Abstract

Pre-pandemic, each year more than 4000 churches close their doors while only 1000 new churches open in their place. Recent research has revealed that one in five churches in America will perinatally close because of COVID-19 on already declining churches. How can the church, across denominational lines in North America get in the middle of this digressing trend, and stem the tide of systemic church decline? *The Post COVID Church* leverages decades of empirical ecclesial work with the fresh perspective of strategic leadership. *The Post COVID Church* will empower the reader to understand causality of a plateau and decline through the lens of the post-modern and post COVID landscape, to recognize the type of new change that proliferates health and growth. *The Post COVID Church* will take church leadership and laity where it needs to go and make strategic transformations in such a way as to not lose those who have held the church together for years. Through the lens of organizational strategy, understanding values, design thinking, leadership development and strategic foresight, *The Post COVID Church* will lead the reader to leverage creativity and innovation toward building momentum again and leading the church to prosper. *The Post COVID Church* is a process that "Socratically" takes the leader and the laity on a journey of discovery and empowerment through strategic leadership.

About Dr. Chris Foster
and This book

The Post COVID Church is an essential resource for leaders desiring to recover from the destructive force of a pandemic and successfully refocus on the mission Jesus left for all His followers. Dr. Chris Foster skillfully compares lessons he learned during his personal health journey to principles he found successful in equipping a church to reach its full Kingdom potential. I took copious notes for my personal files, and I suspect you will too. This book will not be one you read only once. It will become a treasured resource regardless of the organization you lead.

—Alton Garrison, Executive Director, Acts 2 Journey

Dr. Chris Foster has been a long term friend and an example of personal commitment to growth as well as bringing others along a journey they would not have taken without him. I have observed his launching and growing a church to revitalizing the current church he is in. He is a man of passion, purpose and brings significant insight and research into the current situation of the church in America. I meet so many people who do not want to pursue the knowledge of the main issues confronting us but the truth is that ignorance is a dangerous place to live. People are literally destroyed for lack of knowledge and today we see this more than ever. This book is pregnant with information, truth and insight that brings a healthy insight into our circumstances and gives us light to live through it and actually achieve what others have given up on. The man is a friend, the book is incredible and the only thing missing is those who would lift their lid by diving in.

—Maury Davis, author of *Hindsight 20/20*

Dr. Chris Foster offers timely and critical strategies for embracing and flourishing through change in The Post COVID Church. Dr. Foster's writing style and the power of his personal story combine to create a work that is not only academic but a delight to read. This important work has the potential to prepare leaders to turn obstacles into opportunities in advancing the mission of Christ.

—Dr. Kimberly Jones, Vice President of
Southwestern Assemblies of God University

The Post COVID Church

How to lead your church from decline to destiny

by

Dr. Chris Foster

WEBB ·
PUBLISHING

Print ISBN: 978-1-61026-181-4

e-book ISBN: 978-1-61026-207-1

Printed and bound in the United States of America.

Cover design: Debra Dixon
Interior design: Hank Smith
Photo/Art credits:
FoxFire Media and Debra Dixon

:Lcpc:01:

Table of Contents

Dedication

The Post COVID Church is dedicated to my mentor, Pastor, and friend, Dr. J. Don George. As a 17-year-old kid, he brought me onto his pastoral team. When I mentioned to him that perhaps I was too young to serve in that capacity, he looked across his desk, pointed his "preacher finger" at me and said, "Chris, do you ever ask the age of the mailman?" "No", I said. "Why?" He asked. I responded, "Because it doesn't matter, all he is doing is delivering the mail". "Exactly", he said, "I need you to deliver the mail." For the last 31 years, every time I get up to speak, I remember that I am just delivering the mail; the message God sent through His son Jesus on Mt. Calvary.

Pastor had precocious intuition. He had the uncanny ability to spot potential in even the most inconspicuous of carriers, like my-self. I think about it like an apple. Most people chose an apple based upon its external condition. Don George looked beyond the peel to the potential. He saw the seed of possibility in everyone. Because of that there are orchards all over the world that bear his name.

Thank you, Pastor, for your ineradicable passion, thank you for your unimpeachable character, and thank you for your indefatigable pursuit of excellence, because of that, your ineffaceable legacy cast an indelible shadow over the entire earth. The sun never sets on your life's work.

Thank you for believing in us. Thank you for never giving us an excuse to quit. Thank you for showing us how to love, lead, and live. Though now you are among the great cloud of witnesses in Glory, I seek to live every day in a manner worthy of the Leader God gave me as my life example.

Introduction

The surgeon said, "You have the hip of a 75-year-old man." Those words cut deeper than the scalpel he would later wield to remedy the source of the problem. At 37 years of age, I sat speechless in the Orthopedic surgeon's office. The words of the joint specialist seemed to paralyze the more than 7000 synaptic connections of my brain as I slumped in the hard-plastic chair, unable to form a thought. I thought I was strong and healthy. I was running 28 miles per week and feeling pretty good. However, it had become more and more painful to run. I started with two anti-inflammatories, then four, but by the time I had seen the doctor I had to take six just to pull off an eight-mile run. Painkillers are an excellent temporary tool but only mask the problem and seldom ever solve it.

I just thought I was getting older and rationalized that the pain was part of the process, so I needed to look intrinsically and elicit a way to plow through the pain. However, what I did not know is that I was tilling through the utility lines of strength and energy. Bone spurs from a congenital condition were further calcifying to a serrated point, like a saw-toothed blade in my hip socket; it was cutting the remaining cartilage until all was left was a bone-on-bone connection. I went from experiencing pain while I ran to not being able to walk without a pronounced limp.

Although there were pain and other symptoms to let me know that something was wrong, no amount of corporeal assimilation could prepare me for the words of the physician. I sat, overwhelmed in an examination room as the surgeon delivered the crushing description as to why I could no longer run or even walk without an exaggerated limp. Then he showed me the x-ray, saying, "It is as bad as it gets; the only solution is a total hip replacement." On October 3, 2012, I checked into Mayo Clinic in Jacksonville, FL and would check out 14 days later with a new hip, but not without months of rehabilitation and physical therapy. I went from a hydraulic lift to a wheelchair, to a cane, and eventually, I could stand up strong again without pain. Many times, it takes pain to rid your body of pain.

The Apostle Paul coined a profound analogy regarding the church in 1 Corinthians 12:27 stating, "All of you together are Christ's body, and each of you is a part of it." In this chapter as well as in the book of Romans, Ephesians, and Colossians, Paul leveraged the metaphor of the church being the body of Christ. Jesus is the head, and his followers are parts of the body of Christ. Have you ever had the thought, *if the church is the body of Christ, what is the current health condition of His body?*

In North America in the last several decades across denominational and non-denominational lines, the trend of church plateau and decline has grown from marginal to major. Churches that once were lighthouses to their communities are now libraries, mere shadows of the vision of yesterday. Churches that once overflowed with passion and people are now limping by one weekend at a time. Rainer (2005), states, "Eight out of ten of the approximately 400,000 churches in the United States are declining or have plateaued" (p. 35). This alarming avowal is often cloaked by the excellent church growth stories of a few mega churches in densely populated areas. Can this overwhelming trend of church decline be reversed in time to preserve the effectiveness and relevancy of the church in North America, and as such, the quality of leaders she produces for both the ministry and the marketplace?

Compounding an already bleak condition of church health was COVID-19. I remember well having to call my board in on a Sunday night and tell them, we must discontinue live services. By March of 2020, I had only been at City Church for 10 weeks. During that time, we had doubled our attendance, but now everything was different. We went to an online only format for two and a half months. When we opened back up in

June of 2020, in-person attendance was right where we started.

Some of the worse effects of COVID weighed emotionally on pastors who were leading through the most difficult season of their lives. Nearly 40% of all pastors during 2020-2022, seriously considered leaving the ministry permanently. According to Barna Group research, "Over 20,000 pastors left the ministry and 50 percent of current pastors say they would leave the ministry if they had another way of making a living."

In addition to the emotional exhaustion of leading through the unknowns of an ever-changing pandemic, there was the spiritual fallout for church leaders. Prior to COVID, pastors received two types of affirmation. Active affirmation is someone saying "Pastor, you can't make me laugh like that in your sermons I just had surgery", or "I'm selling my boat to pay down the church mortgage," those are active affirmation. Then there is passive affirmation. Passive affirmation is people in the seats. In March of 2020, all of that went away instantly. Next pastors begin to find passive affirmation substitutes. Some of these were harmless and some very harmful. I spoke with a mainline denominational overseer in Georgia who said he had removed 16 pastors during the pandemic for infidelity. What was happening? The passive affirmation had been abruptly removed so some self-medicated with affirmation of another kind.

From the emotional spiritual, and physical exhaustion of pastors today, to the struggling returns of congregations to pre-pandemic attendance, COVID has created some complex challenges. Not dissimilar to my condition before my hip replacement, the church in North America today is limping. It, too, is experiencing some pain and symptoms that are too real to ignore. What would it look like if I were to take an x-ray of the body of Christ in America? Would it reveal a flawless picture of health? Alternatively, would the x-ray show the source of pain, atrophy, and decline? Can the church recover from an undiagnosed trauma that lurks beneath the skin of her often-outdated approaches and paralyzing praxis?

Chapter One

The Limping Church

X-Ray

A roentgenogram, or an x-ray, is essential to finding the real causality of pain and problems in the body. Light is a form of electromagnetic radiation. Some wavelengths take the form of visible light, as seen from a flashlight. Other wavelengths, like the x-ray, are shorter, thus having the ability to penetrate soft tissue such as skin, but not short enough to infiltrate denser material such as bone. When the calcium in the bone stops the x-ray, it forms a shadow, like how a hand will create a shadow when held in front of a flashlight. The shadow from the x-ray transfers to the film or digital processor. In essence, to see through the façade of the skin, it requires a different type of light.

Likewise, *The Post COVID Church* will be utilizing a different spectrum of light, strategic leadership. Strategic leadership will pierce the soft tissues of the organizational system we call the modern church and looking for structural and organizational maladies that will help you as pastors and church leaders, lead your church back to health and your communities back to Christ.

An x-ray allows the physicians to look beyond the façade, to determine causation. Church façades have existed as long as ecclesial leadership. When God gave his law the second time to Moses on top of Mount Sinai, he did so under cover of smoke and fire, through the grandiloquent display of trumpet blasts, thunder, and lightning. Anyone other than Moses who tried to climb the mountain during that time would die. The awe-inspiring mind-blowing miracles that God had performed on behalf of the Israelites to this point in the narrative were to show God's newly freed people that He was mighty. The atmospheric aesthetics on top of Mount Sinai were to show God's people that He was holy.

One cannot spend time with the God of all creation without it affecting his or her countenance. In Moses' case, he was miraculously sustained on top of the mountain through a forty-day fast. Thus, when Moses came down from the mountain, his face glowed. We are not talking about the kind of radiance a person can get as a result of a facial. Moses did not get a facial he got a "faithal." We are talking about the kind of glow that a solar panel can produce through an LED light. Moses got so close to the holiness of God that for a time, God's deity was left on Moses' humanity. The net effect of Moses' time with God was that Moses' glory was so bright the Israelites feared to look at him.

However, after the display of God's holiness, the Israelites did not want God to speak to them directly; they were too afraid, so they asked Moses to deliver God's message. Nevertheless, when the people saw Moses' face, they would not look at him either. Exodus 34:29 says, "When Moses came down from Mount Sinai carrying the two stone tablets inscribed with the terms of the covenant, he wasn't aware that his face had become radiant because he had spoken to the Lord."

So, Moses developed a solution that would allow him to speak to the people directly without the people of Israel seeing his face. Moses covered his face with a veil. He would subsequently take the veil off to go into the tent of meetings, but then he would cover his face back up when he went back out again. The veil served the temporary purpose of mitigating the fears of the Israelites. However, because of the veil the people never knew when the glory of God faded. The veil, in some regard, became an ecclesial façade.

Moses' veil is not mentioned again until Second Corinthians chapter three. Here, the Apostle Paul is doing a comparative analysis of the old and new covenants. Paul juxtaposing the old covenant and the new covenant enumerates the transcendent qualities of the new covenant stating the old covenant was written on tablets of stone, the new covenant was written on the hearts of men. While the old covenant brought condemnation, the new covenant brought righteousness, and the old covenant had a glory that faded, the new covenant has a glory that will never fade. In the midst of that contrast, Paul brings Moses' veil into the epistle with verse 13.

Second Corinthians 3:13 states, " We are not like Moses, who would put a veil over his face to prevent the Israelites from seeing the end of what was passing away." Paul seems to provide parenthetical commentary on the evolved purpose of the veil for Moses. As the glory faded, the Israelites did not know the veil served " to prevent the Israelites from seeing the end of what was passing away."

What began as a function to fill a need continued as a formality to fill a void.

What are the modern-day veils in the church world? What is an old function that is maintained to cloak the reality that the glory is not what it used to be? What elements of church praxis that began out of need are continuing as a façade? This leadership journey will bring fresh insight and perspective much like an x-ray to a medical condition. So, let's schedule the x-ray and get started.

Before my first hip replacement, I asked the Orthopedic Surgeon, "How long can I put this invasive and life-altering surgery off?" He replied with as much compassion as a world-class surgeon could muster, and said, "You will know when it is time." I immediately thought, what does that even mean? That was the medical equivalent of being told, "It is not you; it is me" from someone you were dating." I chased the doctor out of the examination room door into the hallway, while trying to keep everything adequately covered, so as not to give those in the hallway nightmares; I inquired what that meant, and he said, "When the pain begins to change your personality you have to get this done."

My family and staff took the lion's share of the residual of my escalating pain. My pain causes me to be distant, irritable, and to have a shorter fuse. I had an epiphany one night in Orlando, Florida when after a long day of walking at Disney, I verbally laid into the missteps and perpetual shortcomings of an otherwise innocent waiter whose bad night got worse with my unduly berating of his poor service. After my verbal harangue, my family just looked at me in disbelief and disappointment. At that moment, I knew the pain had begun to change my personality. It was time to make a change.

Churches do the same thing as people when they experience health conditions that increase pain, rob the needed energy for vision, and drain the strength of endurance.

Over time churches change their personalities when they have had seasons of decline and pain. Their perspective unknowingly shifts from offense to defense, from a growth mentality to a maintenance mindset and from an outward focus to an inward focus. A heart-pounding vision is slowly traded for a lullaby of security.

A church's personality is a natural and ongoing disposition towards her community and constituents. The church's personality will determine whether the church is postured to receive or repel those outsides of the confines of the church. Significant change is needed when the pain of the circum— stances of decline or plateau exceeds the pain the church will go through in creating change. It is time for a change when the church's DNA or the informed systems of thought and be— havior goes from an outward focus to an inward focus. Broad compassion is unintentionally replaced with a narrow focus on limiting pain, rather than leveraging its gifts to serve its purpose. This narrowing of the vision and focus often takes the form of inaction.

Pre-surgery, the pain was so great that I had to shift the majority of my weight to my good leg; this inaction led to atrophy in my bad leg. Atrophy is the wasting away of size and strength of a part of the body usually as a result of not being used. I remember looking down at my legs in shorts one day, and I was shocked. I had not noticed over the months of favoring the good leg, that the leg that needed the surgery had substantially shrunk in size.

The same thing happens in the body of Christ. When pain, albeit financial, relational, or emotional, hinders the church from using part of its body, atrophy sets in shrinking the capacity for strength. Before long that inaction becomes noticeable in the size and strength of the church. Atrophy happens so gradually that most in the church will not even notice the incremental change until one day, it will have a side-by-side comparison of where it is to where it was, and that perspective will drive the church to cultivate needed change.

It is Time

The church was in a perpetual pattern of decline prior to COVID. Olson (2008) provides an overview of the decline of the Christian church by referencing that 47 percent of Americans attended church each week in 2005, with the average attendance of Protestant churches being 90 adults. Wilson (2016) states that median church attendance by 2012 was 60, with only 10 percent of churches averaging more than 350 people in attendance. Church attendance has been on a decline in America since 1962, which happens to be the year the Supreme Court removed prayer from public schools. At the current rate of church decline, by 2050 only 11% of America's population will be in church. The harsh reality is 80% of those who get saved in North America do so before the age of 18. There is an ever-growing decline of young people attending church. When two trends collide, they form what foresight analysts call a super trend; this is a super trend the church cannot afford to ignore.

Not only were the two trends colliding to form a super trend, but then that super trend merged with COVID. COVID was like a skip button on businesses and churches alike. Churches that may not have established an online presence until another five years, went online overnight, churches that may not have closed for another five years closed during the pandemic. However, the pandemic also opened many new and exciting opportunities for the church to embrace as well, which we will discuss at length later.

The statistics are shocking to see. You may go through some of the same emotions, and processes that I did when I first learned of the severity of my physical diagnosis. You may even go through the full gamut of grief stages as defined by Ross and Kessler, denial, anger, depression, bargaining, and then finally acceptance of this reality.

In Thom Rainer's must-read book titled, *An Autopsy of a Deceased Church*, he states, "Slow erosion is the worse type of decline because the members have no sense of urgency to change." For me, I had grown so accustomed to the slow erosion of quality of life and the increase of pain that I did not see my digression as being urgent enough to demand change. It was only as my surgeon's words came back to me in the parking lot of Wolfgang Puck's in Orlando that I knew the erosion of the quality of life had changed my personality, and it is now time to do something about it. Through this transitional period of pain, the church begins to take painkillers to endure even basic functions of the ministry.

Painkillers

Analgesic, is a group of drugs used to relieve pain. These drugs function in a variety of ways and affect the peripheral and central nervous systems. There are two classes of analgesics, opioids and over the counter painkillers like Ibuprofen. Opioid painkillers work in two ways. Opioids work to interfere with and block the pain transmitters to the brain then go to work in the brain to alter sensations of pain. These drugs do not kill pain but rather nuance the perception of pain. The subsequent sensation augments reality to create a welcomed distraction for the pain sensors. I did not take this type of drug until after the surgery.

Graphic Content Advisory: If you are unfamiliar with a hip replacement, they cut through all of the muscle and completely through the femur bone of the affected hip. Then the surgeons rotate the nearly severed leg 180 degrees and bore a hole down into the femur with a drill that I am sure looks like something Darth Vader would use. Next, they cement the anchor of the prosthetics down into the bored hole, screw the top of it in the hip socket, grind down all of the bone spurs and close the patient up with 30 staples.

One night while in the hospital, I woke up screaming in gut-wrenching anguish, the worst pain I have felt in my entire life. All of the muscles they had cut through were cramping and kept contracting tighter and tighter. A team of nurses rushed into my room and opened the "happy locker," a special safe in the SICU room that held the strongest opioids available and ejected the meds right into my IV. Within seconds this pharmaceutical solution distracted all the pain sensors in my mind and lured me back into a medical utopia. The medicine did not stop the cramping; it simply convinced my pain receptors that everything was okay.

The second type of painkillers is anti-inflammatory; they can be bought over the counter. Ancient Egyptians, chewing on Myrtle Bush leaves, first discovered this kind of analgesic. The Europeans chewed willow bark, and the Native Americans did the same with Birch bark. In the 19th century, pharmacologists identified the common properties of all these ancient remedies as being Salicin. Other more effective derivatives of this chemical have been found and leveraged today.

When you take an Ibuprofen today, it goes to the source of the pain. When cells are damaged, they produce an enzyme called cyclooxygenase. This enzyme produces a chemical that sends pain signals to the brain. Next it releases a cushion type chemical from the blood to further protect more cells from being damaged, thus, the swelling you see around an injury. This kind of painkiller searches the body for cyclooxygenase; then it binds to the enzymes inhibiting the pain signal from getting to the brain. Whether Opioid or anti-inflammatory, neither one solves the problem, they only disrupt the pain messaging system of the body to provide temporary relief.

Much like these painkillers, there are analgesics in the ecclesial world that work not to change the source of the pain but rather to block messages of pain. Therefore, the issues are postponed and compounded. When I started taking more and more painkillers to go on a run, I was further hurting my body. I had the wrong outlook on pain. I was looking to veil the problem as opposed to mitigate it. Pain is our body's way of telling us *Hey, stop doing what you are doing; something is wrong.* The mask of the pain messages allowed me to run further, and with each pound of the pavement, I was destroying the remaining cushion for my joint. Pain is not something to cover up, but rather as a motivator to elicit some change; where there is pain something needs to change.

As a pastor for more than 31 years, I know there can be a tremendous pain in ministry. COVID has compounded that pain. Pain comes through the betrayal of trusted people in our lives; through the constant emotional pull that ministry has on a family. Pain comes when unsuspecting circumstances or uncooperative parishioners mock your best effort. Peter Drucker observed that the four most stressful jobs in America are "president of the United States, a university president, a hospital CEO, and a pastor."

I know the pain of pouring into someone only to have him or her take the knife you used to cut their steak and stab you with it. I know the pain of having to fire staff for indiscretions, and the pain of must let staff go because of economic downturns. I know the pain of having to be "on" residually, and appearing happy about it, even while internally battling depression and the thought of walking away elicits more hope than does the idea of keeping your hand to the plow.

Dr. Samuel Chand in his book *Pain*, states, "For pastors, ignoring pain is leprosy. It may promise a short-term gain of avoiding discomfort, but it has devastating long-term effects" (Kindle location, 510). Chand goes on to say, "Your reluctance to face pain is your greatest limitation" (Kindle location, 564). Chand classifies organizational pain in three categories, "external challenges, internal stresses, and growing pains" (Kindle location 581).

How would you categorize the pain you are feeling in your church today? If you were to give your pain a number from one-to-ten, one being barely noticeable, ten being unbearable, what number would you give the pain from external challenges? External problems would be difficulties outside the church that affect your operational or missional functionality. External pain could be anything from your local economy to a poorly timed real-estate deal just before the market crashed, to a nation reeling from the fear of COVID.

On a scale of one-to-ten, what is your pain level as it relates to internal stress? Internal pain could be dissension, and disunity among the staff, and board, the nauseating pain that comes from a team member's moral failure or competing agendas within the power structure of the church. On a scale of one-to-ten, what is your pain level as it relates to growing pains? Have you maxed out your building, but can't see a way to add another service or expand the facility? Are you teetering on edge between needing to hire a staff member to grow and having the resources to hire that employee? Church pain is real, and leadership pain is real. There are a variety of things both leadership and laity do to kill the pain in a church.

When it comes down to it, painkillers never fix the problem

they only mask the pain. The same is true with organizational painkillers. The main categories of organizational painkillers are programs, perspective shifts, and priority shifts. While at face value they can be good to bridge the gap between the tolerances enduring and delaying unless the real problem is dealt with, they bring no permanent solution. If the pain is ignored, it could even cause more pain.

Programs

Programs are never the problem. However, a program is not necessarily the solution. A good program can become a bad painkiller. If a program is successful in participation, regardless of the purpose fulfilled, if it generates either excitement or revenue, that program can shift the effort of the church away from an outward focus to an inward focus. This over time has a personality-changing effect upon the church. Programs should always support the Great Commission and never distract from it. When a church is reeling from pain externally, internally, or because of growing pains, it is essential to do a fresh evaluation of all of its programs to determine their centrality to the core strategies of the church.

COVID has been a great reset opportunity for churches to nuance their methodology to match their missiology.

At the heart of any painkiller is messaging. As a pastor, I understand the notion to focus on what is working. However, it is also important for leaders and laity to define the term "working." For example, did my six anti-inflammatories work to mitigate my pain so that I could run? Yes, but at what cost? I was merely veiling the pain message and only further damaging the cartilage in my hip. So, you have to get your whole team together and prayerfully decide what is indeed working. In this time of introspection make sure to look at all programs through the lens of the purposes of the church. Just because a program is successful, does not mean it addresses the real causality of pain, plateau, and decline.

Perspective Shifts

Perspective shifts can be a painkiller. A perspective shift can move the eyes of the church from focusing on the one who is lost to an emphasis on the 99 on the hill. A perspective that does not strategically align with the chief biblical purposes of the church can redirect or distract the pain messages of the body and as such, veil or mask the pain as opposed to fixing the pain. Perspective shifts could be the rewarding of a less aggressive agenda because it is budget friendly. An unhealthy perspective shift punishes the risk-worthy types of ideas that got the church to a place of relevance in the community rewarding the "safer" approaches to what drives the church. A perspective shift may suggest, "Instead of going on a mission trip this year, why don't we take a bus trip with our senior citizens?" While there is nothing wrong with a bus tour, when the reason for shifting focus is what is easier, or economical, or upon what would make a few happy, then the perspective shift is serving as a painkiller, thus confusing the messaging of the body. From then on if the church is not careful, she can become dependent upon such painkillers to the extent where the sight or the vision for the biblical function is replaced by a need for an analgesic.

Priority Shifts

The church's priorities are God's principles, God's people, and then God's property. Over the last two and a half decades I have seen these priorities shift to the path of least pain. During the pandemic, there was an even more drastic shift toward rendering many churches with a nearside vision, seeing well close, but not far away. When the principles of God for the church, such as making disciples and going into all the earth and preaching the gospel become painful, there is a priority shift to the next category. God's people become the most important priority for the church. While this will fill the disciples the church already has with knowledge about the Bible and contentment toward the church, it will also create a distance in the relevance toward the lost and the needy of the community. Like the Dead Sea only has inlets and not outlets, churches that shift the priorities away from disciple-making to disciple keeping will ultimately end up with a lifeless pool of overeducated and under-involved church members.

When pain begins to arise in the category of God's people, the priorities shift to God's property. At that point, the pristine condition of the church facility is the most important priority. For example: the idea of bussing kids in from the government-subsidized housing districts becomes objectionable solely based upon what it could do to the facility. The priority has shifted from the principle of evangelism to the people of the church to the property of the church.

Notice with each change in priority comes a pursuit to control more of the outcome. Attention is redirected from the costly and often painful effort of evangelism to keeping the 99 on the hilltop happy, to making sure the barn is clean. These priorities provide a substratum for each subsequent priority. If the property is placed before people, then eventually you will not have the people to support the priority. If keeping disciples is put before making them, then eventually you will not have the disciples to keep. This inversion of priorities is seen today as many churches enjoy immaculate facilities, but they are a dozen funerals away from closing the doors.

This priority shift can be an indicator as to what phase of church decline a church finds itself in currently. If a church has moved maintaining disciples above making them, then they are taking anti-inflammatory painkillers to mask the pain. If, however, the number one priority has shifted from maintaining disciples to the maintenance of the facility, then the church is utilizing opioid painkillers and is more desperate for change, even though often they are most resistant to the needed change.

These priorities do not support themselves if they are out of their biblical sequence. When a church is shifting priorities, she is applying the message-changing process that painkillers use.

The church will never be healthy if her priorities are misaligned. To be clear, all of these priorities must be main–tained. It is the order of the priority that provides the symbiotic relationship to support the subsequent priority. You can make disciples without a church facility, but you cannot adequately maintain a church facility in the long run without the priority of God's principles above God's people. While it is essential that we retain all three of these priorities when a priority shift takes place it removes effectiveness of the symbiosis that makes for a healthy church.

Conclusion

The church in the United States is limping, after COVID, like never before. Statistically, her vital signs are weakening. Sustained pain due to a lack of organizational health can even-tually change the personality of the church. Once the personality begins to change, it starts to cause the church mis–sion to erode along with the number of people that mission is serving. When the personality of the church begins to change it is time to take action. Change is painful, but it is not as painful as allowing the personality to switch to an inward-focused church.

Painkillers can be helpful. They can get us through some difficult times. Painkillers only change the pain messages and don't do anything to address the problem. Whether in a human body or the body of Christ, analgesics will only mask the pain. Painkillers can be a program that changes the pain messages, or a perspective or priority shift. However, real systemic change and organizational health come from acknowledging that the time to change is now.

Organizational experts Cameron and Quinn (2011) note, "If an organization does not change it will die. During the last decade, 46 percent of the Fortune 500 dropped off the list, because they refused to change." The fact is our physical bodies are always changing. The moment a human body ceases to change is the very moment it begins to die.

The largest proprietor of overnight accommodations in the world, Air B&B does not own a single hotel. The largest and fastest growing cab company in the world Uber does not own a single car. The world is changing at a breakneck pace. If the church is not taking a serious look at her health, and approach to the changing world, then it will find itself in the "pain game." The "pain game" is trying to redefine success instead of doing the work Jesus called us to which is to be the Light of the world, the city on a hill and the salt of the earth. Jim Collins (2002) wrote, "The secret to an enduring great company, is the ability to manage continuity and change-a discipline that must be consciously practiced, even by the most visionary of companies." The church should have stability in a firm inner core and the willingness to change and adapt everything except that core. When the church has immovable priorities and undaunted perspective, then she will be positioned to be part of the next surge of church growth, because it is coming.

Chapter Two

Revisit Your History

The Post COVID Church will be leveraging a tool that from here on will be referred to as R.E.F.O.C.U.S. Each sequential step is a letter of refocus and will walk you through a process that when completed will give your church the strength and power to rise above the current trend, and residual adverse effects of COVID. The first step is Revisit Your History.

John the beloved was marooned on the Island of Patmos because the oppressors of the church could not silence him. Tradition says they tried to boil him alive; he was lowered into a vat of oil. However, instead of screams of anguish, the on–lookers heard songs of praise rising emanating from the steam of the boiling drum. God supernaturally preserved his life. In a New Testament sequel to the three Hebrew children, not a hair on his head was singed.

John's tormenters were too afraid of him to keep him, so they dropped him off on this deserted Mediterranean paradise. Revelation 1:10 provides the setting for the letter John wrote to the seven churches of Asia. John was worshiping on the Lord's Day when the Lord himself joined him. I love the fact that John had "church," all by himself. Talk about feeling isolated. Talk about feeling forgotten. There are few things lonelier than ministry; yet here is John, still having church even when nobody else was showing up. The Post Pandemic church can relate to John's plight.

Jesus could have shown up any time of the day or week. How–ever, Jesus showed up at church. If you have been struggling with a low crowd, be encouraged. Have church. Preach like you were preaching to the biggest crowd on the continent, and you worship like you were about to take the stage at the Global Leadership Summit, and Jesus will always show up.

In the loneliness of this moment, John had an encounter with Jesus. The last time John had seen Jesus was a lifetime ago. He was but a teenager when Jesus looked at Mary and John at the cross and told John to take care of his mother. The last glimpse of Jesus John got was when Jesus ascended into heaven before the Day of Pentecost. I am certain John thought that was the last time he would see Jesus on this earth. I am certain he did not believe Jesus would show up at his church service. Previously Jesus had stated, "Where two or more are gathered there I am." You know John thought; *I do not even have two people who are present.* Jesus was the last person John expected to show up at his poorly attended church service. However, Jesus showed up in all His glory.

Jesus and John had both changed a lot since John saw Jesus step onto a cloud and rise into the sapphire seals of heaven. Now John was old. His dark hair exchanged for gray; his strapping youth had been replaced with a frail stature. Likewise, Jesus had to go through some significant changes. His dark hair now "as white as snow" with eyes like fire. Jesus showed up at John's poorly attended service to give him a prophetic word for the churches of his day. Among the customized coaching Jesus did for each of the churches, Jesus had a specific direction for the church of Ephesus.

Jesus said to this church, "I know all of the things you do. I have seen your hard work and your patient endurance. I know you do not tolerate evil people. You have examined the claims of those who say they are apostles but are not. You have discovered they are liars. You have patiently suffered for me without quitting." (*Revelation 2:2-3, NLT*). You have to love how Jesus starts off this organizational coaching session by saying, "I see you; I know your hard work, I know your faithfulness." Perhaps you have been in a season of sowing and have not yet reaped. Maybe you have been faithful to the Lord and His people. Perhaps you have been doing your best to give your best to God, then Jesus sees you.

Jesus then moves from commending to constructive as any good coach would. He said, in verse four, "I have this com—plaint against you, you do not love Me or each other as you did at first, look how far you have fallen! Turn back to Me and do the works you did at first"*(Revelation 2:4-5, NLT)*. Then in excellent coaching format, Jesus ends with commendation again.

Jesus addressed two aspects of mission drift; love for God and love for humankind as being one faltering dynamic, and the works they did when they first began the church. As we look at our history, we must consider both dynamics, along with the historical works that established the church you now lead in that community. Love for God is mutually inclusive to love for man. In fact, this same author wrote, "If someone says, 'I love God' but hates his brother, he is a liar; for he who does not love his brother whom he has seen cannot love God whom he has not seen."*(I John 4:20, NLT)*. If we love God, we will love our brother.

When we fall away from our love for God, we lose the capacity to love our brother. Central to the work of church revitalization is the questions we must all constantly ask about the genuine and authentic love we have in our hearts. Has that love increased or declined? While there is no measurable way to evaluate our love for God or others, we should all pause to ask the Holy Spirit if we have fallen in our love for Jesus or our love for others. If so, simply follow the words of Jesus and repent. Turn to Him and let His love fill you so you can in return love the people He has called you to lead.

After Jesus deals with the church's love levels, he then challenges the church to remember what we did at first. Much of the resistance toward change either from laity or leadership comes from the notion of what we are currently doing is in some way sacred. However, when we take Jesus' church consulting course, He says, we have to change. In fact, we need to go back and review the things we did at first. However, it is vital to discern the difference between the old way of doing things and the reason for doing things the old way.

The Tabernacle Theory

Jesus led his executive staff to Mount Hermon. There, Peter, James, and John witnessed Jesus having a strategic meeting with Moses and Elijah, two iconic Old Testament and historical figures. Peter, one of the three, speaks up, "Lord, it is good for us to be here; if You wish, I will make three tabernacles here, one for You, and one for Moses, and one for Elijah" (*Matthew 17:4, NASB*). This experience was so much greater than Peter had ever imagined, so he wanted to build a tabernacle and stay at that moment. However, Jesus, in His infinite wisdom, shut him down and declined his construction proposition. Perhaps in Jesus' strategic thinking, he knew if you build a tabernacle around a moment in time, an idea, or a movement, it will narrow the agility and create a sense of having arrived at a pinnacle. This feeling of arrival can shift an organization's strategy from an offensive one to a defensive one. If an organization "tabernacles" a strategy, an idea or a moment then the structure built only serves to protect what got them there, and what went before them, rather than being aware of the opportunities that lay ahead.

When the famed disciple asked Jesus about building a tabernacle, he was relying upon his history. The tabernacle of the Old Testament and Peter's day was a seminal piece of Jewish culture, worship, and overall stability. Peter was viewing the direction and trajectory of the future through the lens of a historical perspective. However, Peter did not distinguish the difference between the old way of doing things and the reason for doing things the old way. In light of what he saw on the mountain, Peter wanted to stay in that moment and place and memorialize it.

When you memorialize what you are supposed to internalize, you fail to mobilize what you need to synthesize.

While much can be learned through understanding history, when an organization "tabernacles," it attempts to build walls around a concept, a business model, a program or a system; a strategy there is an undertone of having arrived. "Tabernacling" a strategy is like cutting off the fuel to a jet mid-flight. Yes, it may keep moving. However, there are troubling times ahead.

The demise of the "tabernacled" concepts can be seen in life cycles of business. For example, Montgomery Ward found his success by being in touch with the needs of the changing clientele during the early 1870's. His concept was not a tabernacle on a mountain of business transfiguration but rather born in the valley of seeing people's needs, thinking outside the box, developing a new strategy, and delivering not just product, but peace of mind. This approach made Ward's one of the most successful businesses in several decades.

However, it was the fortification of this strategy, or the "tabernacling" of this model, that made the executive blind to the changes in society, in the economy, and in the industry, which they had previously redefined. Collins and Porras (2002) state, "Indeed, if there is anyone 'secret' to an enduring company, it is the ability to manage continuity and change" (Kindle location, 101). It is in the balance of the continuity of the values, which built success, and the agility and the ability to change, which also made success that the secret formulas emerge to maintain a trajectory of future success for the long haul.

It was Ward's change that put them on the map, made them profitable, allowed them to expand, have a completive advantage, to be category dominant, and it would be a hesitancy to change that would be their demise. Collins and Porras (2002) further state, "The only truly reliable source of stability is a strong inner core and the willingness to change and adapt everything except that core" (Kindle location, 201).

Church leaders should build tabernacles around our values, but there should be strategic placidity to everything else. The only thing that is ineradicable in a church is its values. At times churches will pull the strategies into the tabernacle of values; duct tape the windows shut and wait for things to go back the way they were when they were on top.

However, strategies were never intended to be sacred. Any time you take something that is strategic and blur the lines between value and strategy you conflate your purpose with your preference. Collins (2001) states, "You must never confuse faith that you will prevail in the end, which you can never afford to lose, with the discipline to confront the most brutal face of your current reality, whatever they might be" (Kindle location 1508). There is a blindness that is involved with "tabernacling" strategies.

As a result of the defensive structuring that the executives of Montgomery Ward's did, they would be blind to at least two major shifts in the economic flow of a changing America. The first one was a retail store. Previous to 1900, the mail-order catalog was a strategy that alone allowed them to have a competitive advantage. So much so, that a watch-seller turned entrepreneur named Robert Sears would emulate the strategy with nation-wide success. However, Ward "tabernacled" this strategy as a sacred non-negotiable business element and would be behind the curve when Sears, and later J.C. Penny's, began building retail outlets.

The second opportunity Ward was blinded to because of this "tabernacling" of strategy was the emergence of malls. This missed opportunity was not only as a strategic way to cultivate customers from other stores but a staple of visibility and relevance to the fastest growing suburban regions of the United States. The perception of relevance and the prominence and visibility in emerging markets were not part of the calculus for Wards. As a result, the unwillingness to read the pulse of the consumer and adjust the strategies without changing its values would slim the margins to the point of no return.

Hoffman & Casnocha (2012) state, "Take intelligent and bold risks to accomplish something great. Build a network of alliances to help you with intelligence, resources, and collective action. Pivot to breakout opportunities" (Kindle location 289). History records that Ward's was surrounded by the best and the brightest. However, the "tabernacling" of strategies at the top punished the innovative and informed thinkers away. Pun–ishing innovation is a message that is communicated quickly and understood clearly throughout an organization.

I am originally from Texas. Among the harsh elements in the rustic countryside is a group of pack hunters called coyotes. They are deadly to unattended cattle in the open country. How–ever, there is a strategy Texas ranchers use that works as a deterrent to the pack hunters. A rancher will hunt a coyote, kill one, and hang him up in a tree. To the one who has never been devastated by the ruthless reign of these predator puppies, this may seem harsh. However, it works.

When other coyotes come through in the evening ready to plunder the sick and the young, the carcass swinging in the breeze is all that is needed for the pack to move on permanently. In a very ominous way, this is what Ward did to those who brought innovative ideas to the top, which were in contrast to the now sacred and "tabernacled" strategies. The executives were hung up, thus stopping the flow of information from the most skilled analysts, to the top. In doing so, Ward was cut off from the pulse of the consumer.

By "tabernacling" strategies then instantly firing and hanging up the executives that first suggested building retail stores, in the early 1900's and transitioning to a mall in the 1940's Ward's was in effect locking in their ultimate demise. Not only were they missing out on being well positioned for two significant changes in the market. What started out as an industry-shaping company would end up losing relevance and eventually solvency because of an unwillingness to nuance the strategies that got them there. In 2001 Wards would close its doors for good. What was once an empire was now an epitaph. The reason? They built a tabernacle around a strategy.

Tabernacles and Fences

As a church leader, you should build a tabernacle around your values, and a wooden fence around your strategies. A fence can be moved when needed, and more importantly a fence can be looked through. A fence is designed for definition. It is intend—ed to define the set boundaries; to keep certain things in and certain things out. However, it can always be moved. A tabernacle, on the other hand, is designed for sacred things; things that don't change, things that don't move. A tabernacle is not something you can easily see through. Strategies belong in the fence, values in the tabernacle.

As demand shifts, trends emerge; the strategies should always be stress-tested against the demands, trends, and markets, which are constantly in flux. Often the strategies and ways of thinking which got you there are not the ones that will keep you there. There will always be a watch salesman named Sears, or a clerk called J.C. Penny, Sam Walton or an online startup named Amazon, people who are not commerce complacent or busi—ness model fatigued. If you cut off the flow of information to and from the demand and supply lines of communication, then you have cut the fuel in a flying jet. Canton (2015) states 50 percent of being future smart is understanding trends, and the other 50 percent is about taking actions, designing innovation, formulating plans and crafting strategies, tactics, and collaborations to shape the future you desire." (Kindle location 202).

The difference between a history lesson and a leadership lesson is the willingness on behalf of the leader to glean and grow from the mistakes of others. While Ward's 130-year company is a marvel of what can happen when great information falls into the hands of a great and daring leader, it is also an ad-monitory tale of what not to do. As you give careful consideration to The Tabernacle Theory, there are several questions to ask, which will save you time, money, and heartache if you listen and learn.

What is sacred? Discover your core values, internalize them, build solid walls around them, and treat them as sacred. How do I react to those who give me the information I do not want to hear? What strategies need to have a fence built around them? How often will I ask tough questions about which strategies need to still be inside the fence, based upon the free-flow of information from those within the ministry?

How can we keep a finger on the pulse of the need within the community? Based on our recent history, what strategies do we need to emulate and what do we need to evaluate? What models exist that may irradiate a path of success? What model needs to be developed to illuminate a path to success?

Why? What? How?

Your "why" is your values, your "what" is your objectives and your "how" is your strategies. In the "why" category you have to sit down as a church leadership structure and answer the *why* questions. *Why* do we do what we do? *What* does the Bible say are the purposes of the church? *What* are the non-negotiables for the church? Mission drift begins to occur when we place the preferences before principles and begin to work reactively as opposed to proactively. *Why* did Jesus die? *Why* did He give us the five-fold ministry? *Why* has God placed us in our community? *Why* has Jesus not come back yet? The answers to the why questions are sacred in their very nature. They are to be in the tabernacle and not changed for the sake of post COVID thinking, cultural relevance, circumstance, opportunity, or threat. Make sure you only have sacred things in the taber-nacle.

The next round of questions that you and your leadership must answer is the "what" questions. What questions are related to your objectives? Now that you know why you do what you do, your "why" informs your "what." If your "why" does not inform your "what" then you are in mission drift.

> **Mission drift is when your activity is inconsistent with your identity.**

It is essential to remember that activity does not equate to accomplishment. The church's activity must be informed by her "why." COVID has given many churches the opportunities to evaluate the "what", to make sure it is still in line with the "Why" in light of all of the changes left by COVID.

The human body is an amazing thing, unparalleled among all of creation. In your body, you have something called Homeostasis. Homeostasis is the goal of your body 24 hours per day, seven days a week, 365 days a year. It is an amazing marvel in which various systems are self-regulated based on the introduction of new vital information (Hardy, 2016). The human body innately shivers when cold, drawing blood away from the skin and producing goosebumps which help to shield external temperatures from affecting the body's internal temperature. All of this is done automatically and naturally to warm up the body so that the body's temperature can remain at 98.6 degrees. Our body is constantly monitoring vital elements such as core temperature. When that core temperature dips when it is cold, or spikes when it is hot, the body goes into involuntary overtime to fight to bring the temperature back to its absolute norm. A church leader achieving a homeostasis flow is a present and profound challenge in an ever-changing world.

As leaders, you have to develop automatic shiver points. As external change is affecting internal organizational or personal objectives, you have to have the ability to systematically pri–oritize your needs, analyze the new information, and adjust accordingly, much like the body when it begins to shiver. However, to accomplish organizational homeostasis, the church has to know the "why" or the vital elements that must be maintained automatically to survive. Your "why" has all the critical information needed to keep the church alive and on her purpose.

Few events have thrown the body of Christ off its homeostasis quite like COVID. The body of Christ is at a shiver-point or sweat-point. The most vital thing you as a leader can do is understand the target core temperature, and what needs to change to get the body back to that core temperature.

Conclusion

The purpose of revisiting your church's history is to re-engage with the innovation of the early years. When church leadership and laity rediscover the "why," placing the values in the tabernacle, then they can begin to take a fresh look at the "what," or the objectives, and the "how" or the strategies. By understanding that strategies are intended to be inside a fence and not a tabernacle then leadership and laity can be willing to change strategies with confidence because in doing so the church is not changing what is sacred.

Be willing to move what is inside the fence or move the fence; never remove a sacred thing from the tabernacle. If you do these things, your legacy will live longer, change faster, and remain competitive in an ever-changing world. The role of the church leader is not to shut down new ideas that compete with existing strategy, but rather to farm those ideas, and cultivate those thoughts of future expansion, all the while establishing the static values.

The question that only you can answer for your church is, *what do we love more, our tradition or the lost?* Stetzer, E., & Dodson, M. (2007) state, "Most churches love their tradition more than they love the lost." Ward loved his catalog more than he loved company, his unwillingness to nuance his strategy would be the ultimate demise of his company. Churches will do the same thing as Wards when they lose sight of the "why." They will misplace their priorities and allow preferences to drive deci-sions instead of principles. The church is closing her doors at a rate that would dwarf Ward closures in the last three decades.

When a church revisits its history, it knows the "why" which informs the "what," which prioritizes it is "how" then it can be positioned to drive the type of change that initiates and sustains growth. Where there is growth, there is health, and the organizational wherewithal to posture the church for a brighter tomorrow.

Engagement Questions:

What is our "Why"?

What is our "What"?

What is our "How"?

What are some preferences that may need to be revisited to maintain organizational homeostasis?

What values must never change about the church?

Chapter Three

E-Evaluate Your Current Condition

COVID brought long-term dynamic and dramatic shifts in cultural, liturgical, and social circles that have reshaped societal norms and brought wholesale change. Part of your evaluation must encompass how that change has affected your church cli–mate. If you brought in a national church consulting team who delivered their executive analysis to you on March 7th of 2020, that paper and the information logged therein is worthless, because 70% of the vital information is incongruent with the present realities. Your evaluation of the harsh realities has never been more salient. You need to lead your leadership team through a new S.W.O.T. analysis. What are our new strengths, our new weaknesses, our new opportunities, and our new threats? COVID has brought an undercurrent of change through all these basic categories of analysis.

Introspection is the tool of the wise and the toy of the fool.

Long-lasting results begin with insightful and honest evaluation. After realizing that my pain was beginning to cause pain to others, I scheduled another appointment with the orthopedic surgeon. He shot some additional x-rays, which revealed my well hip was starting to compress. At this point, any time I would stand I would put my full weight on my good leg.

When I walked, I shifted most of my weight to my good leg, and the doctor showed me the difference between my first x-ray and my most recent x-ray. It revealed that the cartilage in my healthy hip was diminishing due to all my weight on my other leg. The surgeon said, "If you do not have this surgery soon, you would need both hips replaced." That evaluation was the final piece of information I needed to drive my decision to change. However, to come to that conclusion there had to be a profound interaction between the insight of the doctor and honesty with myself. The same is true for the church. If she is going to have an accurate evaluation, it will not happen without a dynamic and honest dialogue between hindsight and insight.

Hindsight

Strategic vision combines hindsight and insight to create fore–sight. Every leader must master those two aspects of visionary sight to create foresight. Hindsight is what is learned or confirmed from past experiences. In hindsight, I never should have sold that 68 Ford Mustang my dad and I restored. In hindsight, I should have bought Starbucks stock 15 years ago. In hindsight, you should not have bought your wife a vacuum cleaner for her birthday. Hindsight.

As Pastors and leaders of the church, it is imperative that we leverage hindsight to understand what has happened to the church in the last several decades, and perhaps more impor–tantly, what has happened in the last few years.

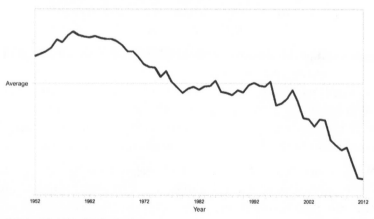

The Great Decline: 60 years of religion in America

Graph by Corner of Church & State, a Religion News Service blog
Source: Aggregate Religiosity Index, J. Tobin Grant. *Sociological Forum.*

Graphics such as this are shocking to see. You may have the same gut-punched feeling I did when the doctor first put up the x-ray of my bone-on-bone hip. Denial is the first passive emotion that emits from the temporal lobe. I remember thinking; *no way is this my hip.* Hindsight starts with honesty to the actual condition. Hindsight ignores the temptation to spin the results to a friendlier narrative. Hindsight forces you to take away the distracting painkilling messages and forces you to deal with present reality. Back to the vacuum cleaner gift illustration, you could have justified the reaction by saying, "I must have caught her on a bad day, or maybe I should have bought a nicer vacuum cleaner." However, hindsight forces you to deal with the real issues at hand.

> ### *The real issue is that a vacuum cleaner is not a gift it is a tool.*

In the case of this declining spiritual trend in America, it cannot be ignored that the downward trend began at the same time the Supreme Court decided to remove Bible readings and prayer from the public schools. On June 25, 1962, the United States Supreme Court decided in Engel v. Vitale that a prayer approved by the New York Board of Regents for use in schools violated the First Amendment because it represented the establishment of religion. In 1963, in Abington School District v. Schempp, the court decided against Bible readings in public schools along the same lines. (Star, 2014). Some will argue there are many other external and internal contributing elements to this shift, and they would be right. However, biblical hindsight demands the acknowledgment of the power of prayer and the fact that the priority of God being normalized into the fabric of our culture has shifted. Therefore, hindsight teaches the church that a revival of his church and a reversal of this trend cannot come until a priority of prayer is implemented.

As pastors and leaders, take some time to evaluate and define what other changes have attributed this national shift in spiritual prioritization. *How has media affected the priority of God for America? How has family structure changed the priority of God in*

America? How has work structure altered the priority of God in America? How has urbanization affected the priority of God in America? Profound and hindsight-driven dialogues about the pattern shifts of America will provide historical backdrop upon which to view church growth or decline patterns. The purpose of hindsight work is not to ascribe blame but to cause leaders to think deeply regarding patterns and cultural shifts that have affected the church's perceived relevance in our society. After the church acknowledges pivotal patterns, she can navigate the meta-shifts in our culture, which affect the church.

Insight

Insight is the ability to interpret, prioritize and respond to information in the present.

The next aspect of strategic vision is insight. The leader who is insightful asks many questions and uses the information to inform and transform the present.

Information without formation will lead to frustration.

For this reason, going to another seminar is not necessarily the answer to the challenges you face in your church. While seminars can both inspire and inform, without insight, the ability to assimilate new information and prioritize that new information toward your objectives and your strategies will only frustrate your effort to see a path forward. Solomon wrote, "A prudent person foresees danger and takes precautions. The simpleton goes blindly on and suffers the consequences" (*Proverbs 27:12, NLT*). The church cannot afford to suffer the consequences of not prioritizing information blindly.

Many questions must populate the dialogue of church decline. What has changed outside of your local church in the last ten years? What has changed in the last two years? What has changed economically, socially, politically, and technologically? Take a moment and write a paragraph description of how each of these categories has changed in a way that affects the church. At the end of each section write the answer about what lessons the church is learning from these external changes.

Next, take a look at changes in your church over the last ten years, then two years. What variations have occurred to your "why," "what," and "how," or your values, your objectives, and your strategies? If your strategies for fulfilling your objectives have not moved to meet the changing needs of your com—munity, then ask yourself these questions. *How have the changes in the community affected the needs of the people we are trying to reach? In what ways are our current strategies not meeting the needs of our changing community? What have been the structural, cultural, social, and or economic shifts in my community? How is demographics in my community growing? What does the church need to do to meet the needs of this growing demographic? How has social media changed the way people find a church? How does our social media strategy meet people on that plain of expec-tancy?*

Just as crucial to dialoguing concerning what has changed re-garding your community's needs is what will never change concerning your community's needs. People still love their kids and want them to have every advantage to win in life. People are still in search to fill a God-sized hole in life that only Jesus can fill. Jones (2016) states, "The more you change, the more you need to talk about what will never change" (Kindle locat-ion, 1364). As conversations about change begin, Jones high-lights a staple for Socratic dialogue. The elephant in the room of change is standing on a social distancing dot that reads *the fear of the unknown.* Therefore, by stating emphatically what will never change, it allows people to philosophically or theologically breathe and only then are they able to discuss things that may need to change fully. Once you have had an in-depth dialogue with your leadership teams about these questions, it will begin to reveal an x-ray type image about some of the structural and perhaps even philosophical elements that highlights what change you need to lead.

Money In-sight

It is not impossible to have a holistic evaluation of your church without having a forensic evaluation of your money. This budgetary evaluation is not an audit of where money is spent but merely a direction discovery of the flow of money. What is the direction of your church's budget? Surprisingly, I am not as concerned with the up and down directions as I am the in and out directions of funds. The direction of the money reveals patterns that have predictive connotations to the future posturing of your church. Going into this budget evaluation is touchy. This assessment is never to be a blame-generating discussion. However, through a simple process, I can tell you if your church's money patterns are supportive of your values, objectives, and strategies or if they are undermining those very priorities.

Place an arrow by each line item. Write "<" representing out–ward for every line item that is focused on reaching the community, evangelism, serving the less fortunate, and missions. Next, write ">" for inward for every line item that focuses on maintaining efforts inside the church. While every situation is as unique as the communities and leaders them–selves, if there is a noticeable trend that escalates more "inward" arrows and less "outward" arrows this signpost can formulate an insightful predictive conclusion about your future.

Rainer (2014) states regarding autopsies he performed on closed churches, "More than any one item, these dying churches focused on their own needs instead of others. They looked inwardly instead of outwardly" (Kindle location, 194). Rainer further states, "In dying churches, the last expenditure to be reduced are those that keep the members most comfort–able" (Kindle location, 287). Insightful dialogue about the direction of money in previous years could have changed the destiny of these churches that are now permanently closed. While it is too late for the churches on which Rainer per–formed an autopsy, it is not too late for your church.

So far in the course of evaluation, you have answered questions about what has changed about church attendance in the United States, what has changed about your community, your values, objectives, strategies, and your budget. However, this data is still raw. Raw information, unless it is prioritized toward your objectives and is used to help form your strategies does not transform. Information without prioritization will never lead to transformation. It is as you let the x-ray of historical patterns interact with the dense mass of your cultural and community needs that you can emerge with an image. That image determines how your objectives and strategies need to shift to grow your church in an ever-changing environment. However, there is more data to be collected.

Church Check-up

Once the surgeon showed me an image of my only good hip decreasing in cartilage, it helped me decide to have the surgery. However, other indicators needed to be evaluated to determine my ability to survive and recover from the surgery. As a result, I received a thorough physical and some psychological evaluation. A team of doctors and technicians were probing the measurable elements of my health looking for any areas of concern that would inhibit a full recovery.

Likewise, many factors contribute to your church's health that must be objectively evaluated at this phase of your journey. I have developed a tool that will help gauge the level of health in the five different purposes of the church. Rick Warren wrote *The Purpose Driven Life*, and the *Purpose Driven Church*. Because of the biblical-centric nature of these purposes, they are the industry standard and universal in their application to your church. The five purposes are worship, evangelism, fellowship, discipleship, and ministry. While your implementation style will vary depending on denominational affiliation, community context, and ministry philosophy, these purposes are the "why" behind your "what." Health is never determined by independent systems but rather interdependent dynamics. If I had a healthy brain, but an unhealthy heart, no amount of mental strength could allow me to recover from this surgery. Therefore, health, is defined holistically. However, to determine holistic health, each purpose must be evaluated by the body of believers.

The Church Check-up is just that. It is a way in which you, as a pastor or leader, can determine the holistic health of the church based on the universal and biblical standards for the purposes of the church. In this sense, the purposes are akin to the systems of the body. For this evaluation, you as the church leadership will listen to the body of Christ in your church. A good physician will tell you to listen to your body. Sometimes in the ecclesial world, it is easy to assume you know what the body needs. In doing so, you as a leader run the risk of diagnosing in a bubble.

If your barometer for change is not derived from the whole body, then you could miscalculate simply because your infor-mation is coming from a homogeneous information pool. Additionally, by involving the entire church, you are allowing people to grapple with the health issues of the church and in that process of wrestling with the brutal facts, will be more of an active part of the solution, instead of a passive aggressive part of the problem.

The purpose of this exercise is to determine a holistic health picture. This evaluation is intended to reveal an area of the church health that needs attention. While the assessment is based on 100 percent, the results are not designed to show a pass or fail but rather health indicators that form a dialogue regarding health.

Rate each purpose of the church on a scale of one to ten with ten being the highest with no room for improvement, one being the lowest possible health rating.

Worship

1. How well do we model the significance of worship in weekend experiences through music and song?

2. How well do we model the importance of worship in weekend experiences through prayer?

3. How well do we model the significance of worship through the sermons?

4. How well is worship incorporated into other departments of the church such as children's ministry, youth ministry, discipleship, and other auxiliary ministries?

5. How well is the importance of worship presented to visitors and new attendees?

Section total _____ x 2=_____

Fellowship

1. Rate how well the sermons reflect the importance of fellowship.

2. Rate the number of opportunities for fellowship.

3. Rate the quality of opportunities for fellowship.

4. Rate your fellowship experience at church.

5. Rate the communication regarding all fellowship opportunities.

Section total _____ x 2=_____

Discipleship

1. Rate the number of opportunities to grow in knowledge and experience with Christ.

2. Rate the number and quality of small group opportunities for your discipleship experience at the church.

3. Rate how well we prioritize and communicate the need for discipleship through the sermons.

4. Rate how well the discipleship experience is promoted and communicated to the church.

5. Rate how well discipleship is incorporated into different departments (children's ministry, youth ministry, and other auxiliary ministries).

Section total _____ x 2=_____

Ministry

1. Rate how effectively and frequently servant opportunities are made available to the church.

2. Rate how organized servant experiences are at the church.

3. Rate how development and training are accomplished for servant experiences at the church.

4. Rate your experience as a servant leader.

5. Rate how the servant's heart is communicated through sermons.

Section total _____ x 2=_____

Evangelism

1. Rate evangelism in the weekend service experience.

2. Rate how likely you are to bring a lost person to the church.

3. Rate how effective the weekend services are to reaching the lost.

4. Rate how the importance of evangelism is communicated through the sermons.

5. Rate the church's vision as an evangelistic church.

Section total _____ x 2=_____

Once these evaluations have been completed by 60 to 80% of those who attend on a regular basis, the church administrative team will compile the data. Next, the goal is a consensus. Very little disregard should be given to the lowest and highest marks. Instead, you are looking for a clear pattern of church health. For instance, the lowest scores across the whole church are in fellowship, that is not an indictment of the pastor; it is a key indicator that this system is not healthy. If evangelism is low, then the way the church is communicating and doing evangelism is not healthy. The Church Check-up provides a means by which all people in the church can join the conversation and communicate what hurts in the body.

Once the church leadership has determined which purpose of the church is in need of treatment, then measures can be discussed and implemented to treat the affected purpose incrementally. Olson and Eoyang (2011) indicate, "Rather than focusing on the macro strategic level of the organizational system, complexity theory suggests that the most powerful process of change occur at the micro level where relationships, interactions, small experiments, and simple rules shape emerging patterns" (Kindle location, 259). The treatment for low evangelism scores begins with a sermon series followed by small group sessions with an opportunity to execute a community outreach. Then the change has to get from the initiative phase to the internalized phase, but this process is incremental and intentional.

Ackermann and Eden (2011) state, "Effective organizational change relies upon incrementalism, upon many small wins, rather than one big win" (p.9). Actual enduring change happens daily, not in a day. Daily change can be observed on the physiological level by observing diet patterns. Crash diets never last because people still think the same way about food and or working out. It is the incremental lifestyle changes that render transformation such as the commitment to never eat after 7 PM or stop drinking calories.

In the same way, the treatment must evolve into a way of life for the church. Treatment cannot be viewed as an option; it must be seen as the only alternative. The surgeon told me, "After surgery, physical therapy is not an option." In the same way, once an area of church health is identified as being in jeopardy, the solution that is derived must be prioritized and the way church life was lived before it was changed to meet the treatment expectations of the area in need. Other than a healthy, holistic conversation and reengagement, the most significant emotion that is derived from this type of evaluation is urgency.

When urgency is lost, standards fail; best intentions are exchanged for poor excuses, principles are exchanged for preferences, and insights fall into the vortex of self-interest. Urgency is the driver of change and the sustainer of strategic paradigm shifts. With urgency, vision can transform, inspire, and lead change. Without urgency, vision dies, and according to the Bible "Without a vision, people perish" (*Proverbs 29:18, KJV*).

Foresight

We have all heard that hindsight is 20/20. However, it takes more than hindsight to create a perfect strategic vision.

Hindsight married with insight, produces foresight.

Hindsight is the rear-view mirror, insight is the dashboard oncoming traffic, road signs, and weather conditions, and foresight is looking through the windshield with proper interpretation of hindsight, and insight. All are necessary to drive your vision forward. Foresight is the ability to predict and prepare for the future. Foresight is derived from prioritizing and accurately interpreting information at the hindsight and insight levels. These two organizational optical nerves funnel prioritized information through the grid of your strategies, objectives, and values. Foresight can determine how well your strategies will fulfill your objectives in the future based upon predictable and knowable patterns.

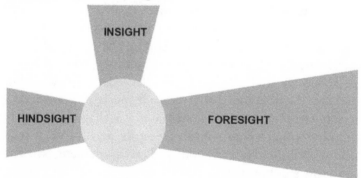

Hindsight lets you learn from your past and insight allows you to accurately interpret your present realities. If you or your leadership is unwilling to honestly interpret hindsight, then no amount of strategic acumen can guide your organization toward a bright future. However, when those two elements of strategic vision are forced through the grid of why, what, and how, or your values, objectives, and strategies, then you will have the perfect strategic vision. The vision that is void of hindsight and insight is blind to the future. That organization will repeat the mistakes and missteps of the past, ignore the warning signs in the present, and not be in a position to pounce with agility on the opportunities of tomorrow.

Foresight work is quite complex. It requires the full knowledge of patterns in the past and present, and the ability to separate a pattern, a trend, and a cycle. A pattern has set parameters. No matter what comes along, the result of a pattern will be the same. In tailor work, regardless if the fabric is cotton or velvet when you cut around a pattern, it will always end up the same. A pattern has to do with the limits or proclivities of a leader or an organization. A pattern has to do with inside sources affecting the outcome. A pattern can change but only with an actual change to the structure of the organization. This structural change may be a transition in leadership or a transition within a leader who is hungry for results.

A trend has more to do with outside forces contributing to the outcome. Whereas a cycle is related to patterns interactions with trends when the influx of the trend exceeds the structure of the pattern, there is a bubble pop and subsequent rebound which ultimately repeats. The cyclical process can be witnessed in the painful housing crash of 2009. Cyclical dynamics are seen in all free market expressions. It is no different with the church.

Conclusion

Evaluation is the fuel for informed strategic change. Without honest and insightful evaluation, a pastor will be tempted to attend a conference and go back home and attempt to replicate what one successful church did in a particular area. While on-site studies I contend are the best process to learn what works in the context of the church you are studying, a pastor or leader cannot copy and paste someone else's strategies without considering the full context. What works for a non-denominational church in Dallas will not work for a denominational church in Delaware.

Evaluation seems risky for the present leader, and therefore many who seek to preserve his or her position will erroneously resist engagement in the process. However, pastors and leaders must recognize that the riskiest thing to do is nothing. The scariest thing to face is not your history it is your Maker. It is vital to realize God is on your side, and if you lead through this process, history will be on your side as well.

Evaluation is the effort of the prudent. Evaluation says I want to learn from the past and the present so that we as a church can be prepared to optimize the future. Start by asking yourself a series of questions.

Engagement Questions

Outside the church: How has my community changed in the last ten years, how has it changed since COVID? What is the naturally growing demographic of those in a five-mile radius of the church? How does this data inform the objectives and strategies of the church? What is changing socially, economically, technologically, and politically in our community that affects the church? What has changed inside our church the last ten years?

Inside the church: Place arrows on the flow of your money for the last decade. What patterns do you see related to what direction the money is going? Are there more inward arrows and less outward arrows than there were ten years ago? Are we spending money in conjunction with the strategies that meet our objectives? Next, lead the church in a Church Check-up. What is the lowest-scoring purpose of the church? What are some measurable ways the church can structure growth and improvement in this area? How do we build urgency to bring this area back to health? What lessons can we learn from hindsight dialogue? What information do we need to consider for insight dialogue? What are some of our church's patterns, trends, and cycles? How can we as a church prioritize our hindsight, and insight to create foresight? What type of future do we want for the church? What are some specific elements that we want to see in our future church? Finally, if Jesus were evaluating our church, what might He say needs to change?

Chapter Four

F-Formulate a 12-Month Attractional Missional, Hybrid Calendar

Among the emerging trends that arose from the pandemic, zoom meetings became the new norm for pastors and leaders to connect and communicate as we sought to navigate the ever-changing realities. I was asked to speak on a national zoom conference to help get pastors unstuck from the post quarantine lull. I covered a couple of philosophical shifts about which we as leaders need to pay attention, and then I sent the last part of my talk helping leaders strategize about getting people who have stayed away from church since quarantine back into the building with a few attractional strategies.

The very next speaker, a prominent pastor, who was likely not on the call when I was talking came on immediately after me and magniloquently proclaimed "Attractional is Dead"! It would have been more comical if I thought people weren't going to believe him. If the attractional model of leveraging resources, and strategies to get people to come to the church is really dead, then this pastor should sell his 17-million-dollar facility, fire all of the maintenance staff and just do missional work. No chance. Right? This is the era of the hybrid.

> **The church cannot ignore the theology of missional disciplines any more than she can ignore the methodology of attractional contributions to this new normal.**

Cat-a-strophic

Early in the 1950's, there was a deadly emergence of malaria with the Dayak people in Borneo, an island in Southeast Asia. The malaria outbreak was claiming so many lives that the government placed a call to the World Health Organization to mitigate the national health crisis. Malaria is transmitted via the hypodermic proboscis, which serves to extract blood from any warm-blooded animal. Just like diseases can transfer through a hypodermic needle, mosquitoes can spread diseases through their proboscis. The deadly malaria outbreak was a direct result of the out-of-control mosquito population on the island.

The WHO came to this conclusion and made the hasty decision to load airplanes with an insecticide and spray the entire island from the air to mitigate the mosquito predicament. Dichlorodiphenyltrichloroethane or DDT was the weapon of choice for the WHO (1979, World Health Organization). The airplanes flew in patterns blanketing the entire island with the aim of killing the mosquito populace, thus stopping the further spread of Malaria. The plan worked brilliantly; the island's malaria-infected mosquitoes made contact with the copious amounts of DDT and fell to the sand (World Health Organization, 2005).

However, there were some unintended consequences that emerged. Not only did the bombardment of DDT wipe out all of the mosquitos, but it also killed off a particular species of parasitic wasp. The staple food source of the wasp was a type of thatch-eating caterpillars. With the wasp, no longer around to control the caterpillar population, there was an explosion in their population. As a result of the overabundance of thatch-eating caterpillars with no natural predator, thatch roofs, the island's main roofing material for the homes began to fall in on people's heads by the hundreds. In addition to those injured by the falling roofs, there was the danger of being exposed to the elements. When the entire island no longer had roofs other health issues like pneumonia began to plague the island's inhabitants.

Additionally, when the wasps fell to the ground, it was an all-you-can-eat scenario for the geckos, which dominated the lizard population. While geckos are immune to the effects of DDT, the cats of the island, the gecko's main predator, were not immune to the insecticide. Before long, cats began to die all over the island because they ate the geckos that ate the wasps.

With the cats gone, it gave a window for the explosion of one of the cat's chief prey, the rat. Rats multiplied rapidly, which contaminated the grain supplies of the island and led to the plague along with other deadly diseases (O'Shaughnessy, 2008). As a result, this island faced a more significant crisis. Once again, the government of Borneo reached out to the WHO, and they came up with an innovative solution. They loaded crates filled with cats and the United Kingdom's Royal Airforce parachuted the cat-filled containers onto the infected island. The cats curtailed the rat population, and the island was able to work its way to health yet again.

There are several lessons that can be gleaned from this cautionary "tale." However, chief among them is derived from answering this question. How do your solutions affect your ecology? Just like every geological place has a unique ecosystem, so does every organization. Ecosystems are a complex network of interrelated systems. Each system has an interdependent predator to prey, or supply and demand symbiosis. In the case of Borneo, the wasps of the island seemed insignificant until they were removed. The caterpillars seemed innocuous until roofs began to collapse. The DDT seemed effective until the cats began to die. The rats seemed to be held at bay until there were no natural predators. The roofless island population suffered the unintended consequences of treating a unique problem with a blanket solution. From the backdrop of this amazing and true story, it is vital that you think through your unique scenario with system lenses.

On the heels of rapid change and cultural shifts left behind from COVID-19, it's imperative to understand the new "ecology" of your church. What aspects of attractional and missional need to be developed and deployed to build momentum and focus to fulfil the church's mission. Unlike WHO we need to understand the ecology before we go spaying one solution over the mission and mandate of the church.

Colorblind Glasses

I am colorblind. While I can see some colors, I cannot distinguish them. Others have to tell me what clothes match. Sometimes I mannequin shop. I would go to the store and purchase whatever was on the mannequin knowing that I was safe. I look for the position of a traffic light to determine the direction; top, middle, bottom. I have never seen a full rainbow, distinguished the beauty of a butterfly, or been good at playing Uno. Not seeing any color was a way of life, and I had resigned myself to the fact that I would see color as God intended when I saw Jesus for the first time. In that way, it would be an extra blessing.

However, recently some friends of mine sent a package in the mail. I had no idea what was going on. They had purchased a pair of Enchroma sunglasses. These miraculous specs allow most colorblind people to see color for the very first time. I opened a box that had a pair of sunglasses in it. I had not heard of this breakthrough technology, and the brand name did not mean anything to me. I was still a little confused however, I put the glasses on, and suddenly everything was extremely bright. I was looking around at a world I did not recognize. My eyes immediately began to adjust to these lenses, and after about a minute I could for the first time in my life see color.

I wept at the first sunset I saw; it looked like Heaven was kissing the earth. At a zoo, I stared at a peacock for over 20 minutes. Now I follow butterflies around the yard just like my six-year-old little girl. These lenses have changed the way I see the world. Likewise, I am hoping that you can begin to see the world in which you work, through the lenses of systems. When you put the specs on and start to look around, it will change the way you see the world and approach solutions in your own life.

There are ecosystems in your church. There are a supply and demand interdependence that keeps things a certain way. Ecosystems within an organization operate the same way as ecosystems in a geographical location; they are in perpetual motion to maintain a "normal." When one part of an ecosystem is changed, the whole system works through the nuances until the new normal is quickly defined. Interdependent pieces of the ecosystem do not operate in a vacuum, but instead in concert with the other interdependent systems. When the World Health Organization sought a solution to the deadly malaria outbreak, they did not look at the problem with the lens of existing systems that were interdependent, and as a result, it changed an entire ecosystem of the island to the demise of many people's lives.

The Post Pandemic Church does not seek to instigate blanket change over unique and nuanced church settings, but rather to equip you with a pair of system glasses, with which you can see what has been there the entire time. No matter the scope, no matter the scale, your church has interconnected systems that produce a "normal." If that normal is not healthy or productive then change does not need to come wholesale, but rather strategically.

Strategic Change

Strategic change is when an organization is fully aware of its strengths, weaknesses, opportunities, and threats, and makes changes to their internal systems, which produce outcomes that are constant with their objectives. Strategic change happens when those with influence understand that incremental changes have the power to affect the desired outcomes. Next, strategic change seeks to communicate the needed adjustment to the functional and operational levels of the church with vision, clarity, and the permission to fail.

Strategic change is not emotional; it is not reactionary; but instead, it is calculated through the avenues of hindsight and insight. Strategic change is fully cognizant as to how existing systems function and how subtle changes can generate an entirely new set of boundaries; likewise how others can shut down the flow of intrinsic contribution to the church's life, and exacerbate the complications within the church.

Often when we think about change, we think about music style, stage dress, and which translation of the Bible should be used from the stage. While these are elements to consider, the most effective change starts with the philosophy, one that recognizes hindsight, and engages insights. Next, it explores the nuances of existing systems before making a wholesale change decision. Part of the way a strategic leader arrives at this conclusion is by asking "Why" after every point of inquiry. The children's ministry has been the same size for the last three years. "Why?" We don't have a full-time children's pastor. "Why?" We can't afford a full-time leader. "Why?" We don't have enough young families in the church. "Why?" We don't have a full-time children's pastor. The point when the "why" questions cycle back is the nuance that has the most potential to change the desired outcome.

When you chart the "why" behind an ongoing dilemma, it will shed some light on the issue that will bring the most strategic change. If resources are what is needed, and the right person in the right role is the strategic change that would break the cycle, then a capital campaign to add the needed staff member will be the element that redefines the future. The point in which the answer to the "why" question crosses back to the same "because," is the watershed opportunity of strategic change. Once the church leadership has homed in on the actual problem, not the perceived problem, only then will they lead strategic change.

What's Wrong with This Picture?

Never underestimate the power of preconceived ideas. We all have them. They are the frameworks through which we view all matters. I am from Texas. There is a saying that I have heard and often said since leaving the state in 1998, "You can take the man out of Texas, but you can't take the Texas out of the man." This colloquialism speaks to a rugged sense of adventure, a love for the outdoors, a no-quit attitude, and many other presuppositions through which life is viewed. Sometimes those preconceived ideas are latent with strong attributes and other times they are a weakness. Preconceived ideas can be a strength or a weakness depending on the truth that surrounds the notion. What's wrong with this picture?

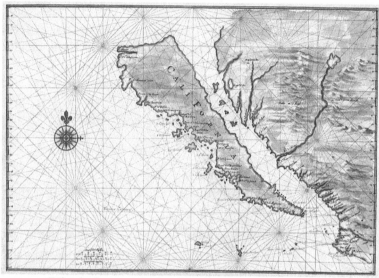

(Vinckeboons, J. & Library of Congress, 1650)

It is confusing, right? It may come as a surprise to you, but this was the greatest cartographic mistake in the history of the world, and it all stemmed from false underlying assumptions. The Spaniards were exploring the Baja Peninsula, and after navigating North for a while, the exploration crew assumed that the bay was, in fact, a river. So instead of proving their hypothesis, they commissioned a team to sail North to find the inlet of the river. They sailed all the way to the Vancouver inlet and began to sail South, past modern-day Seattle. Before long, the crew made the false assumption that the channel was the river and turned around, sending the false presuppositions to Spain to be printed. Since Spain was the authority on map-making for decades, and in some cases, a century, California was believed to be an island.

False assumptions are not unique to cartographical errors. In fact, it is more likely than not that you or someone on your team is reprinting the improperly charted maps of an assumption that was believed by someone who went before them. Strategic change calls for everyone to be willing to question their presuppositions in search of the most vital truths. As leaders, we should all take a "trust but verify" approach to our operating theories that are churning out the current results.

Senge, Kleiner, Roberts, Ross, and Smith (1994) note, "Mental models are the images, assumptions, and stories which we carry in our minds of ourselves, other people, institutions, and every aspect of the world" (Kindle location, 4519). These presuppositions, true or not, either serve to limit or leverage our paths to a strategic decision. A decision is not strategic unless it challenges presumptions or the mental models before coming to a fresh conclusion.

There is a model in accounting called double-loop learning. Single–loop learning centers on finding mistakes and fixing them, thereby maintaining the status quo. Double-loop learning circles once to correct the error and a second time to fix the problem. (Senge, Kleiner, Roberts, Ross, & Smith, 1994). Double-loop learning does not seek what is going wrong; it seeks why it is going wrong, and how to remedy it.

To procure a real solution, one has to dispel his or her conceptions about why things are and seek real causality as to how to repair them. Double-loop learning is proactive instead of reactive. The leader must be willing to learn even at the cost of a presupposed belief. Many leaders have worn their presumed beliefs as a badge of honor all the way down the death spiral of their organizations.

In my hip story, I presumed for too long that my health was good because I could endure the pain of a long run instead of double looping back to what was the causality of the pain. The painkillers did not mitigate the problem but instead exacerbated it. If I had asked questions about my assumptions, then perhaps I would still have my original hip. Failing to challenge your theories-in-use will never lead to strategic change. It will instead, continue decline, increase pain, and keep you further from your desired outcomes.

Questions

What ecosystems are currently at work that affect your church's health, growth, and strength? How can system lenses change how you view the challenges in your church? What are your theories related to the current growth trends in your church? When was the last time you tested those theories to confirm they are not an "Island of California?" What does it mean for your church leadership team to make strategic decisions? How would double-loop learning change outcomes for your church and what are some ways you can loop back to the causality?

In the throes of answering these questions, allow me to review a few critical terms into the conversation. Two fundamental philosophies inform your church's basic assumptions. These two models are the lens through which you view your operational and organizational structures. These two words are attractional and missional. These are two arguments the church world has been theoretically sparing back and forth among varying camps.

An attractional model says the church does certain things that draw people to church, and when they are at church, they will experience a life change, and stay through community resulting in growth. The attractional church may have a big-name Christian artist come in to do a concert. They may throw significant events at the church and inspire people to come. They may have all of their stock in a beautiful facility, believing that the building will draw people into the Kingdom of God.

A missional model focuses on empowering people to send them out to complete the mission of the church. These two terms, missional and attractional are not mutually exclusive. It is not a zero-sum game between the two camps. There are attitudes and actions in each camp that are beneficial to help your church refocus. I have seen the missional camp claim the spiritual high road while dismissing the attractional elements they embrace for their service, facilities, and staffing choices. Likewise, I have seen those in the attractional camp claim the higher moral territory regarding evangelism statistics and church size.

The Churches that look disparagingly on those who do things differently, without exploring the ideas the other camp has that work, are one step closer to irrelevance. The point is, these philosophy frameworks have shifted into entrenched preexisting theological debates, which have little to do with the appropriateness or functionality of the ideas as a whole, especially post- pandemic.

To the missional camp critical of the attractional church, the question needs to be asked, if being attractional is not essential then why mow the churchyard, paint the trim or even have a website? To the attractional camp critical of the missional church, why do discipleship classes? There needs to be a hybrid of all biblical and productive ideas, without a blind eye toward the ideas that can improve the health and vitality of the church.

The Missional Church

Imagine if you moved from America to Asia to be a missionary. While you are excited about the prospect of leading people to Jesus, you are lobbed into a culture that sees the world differently from almost every angle. Not only do you have to navigate the personal adaptation within your family and carve out a new way to live, additionally, but you also have to take all of your methodologies toward ministry in your previous content and suspend judgment on what will work in this ministry setting.

Profound questions would need to be asked and answered in your approach to bringing people to Jesus. You would have to wear system lenses and study the long-established "ecosystems" that make the culture work. The first year in this foreign setting you would spend identifying the most significant needs of the culture and pair those needs with the greatest gifts of your ministry. You would ask more questions than you would give answers. You would learn more than you teach. A failure to approach the new assignment this way would result in frustration and ineffectual endeavors.

Your missiology informs your methodology. Missiology is the study of the way your mission is implemented. Branson and Martinez, state (2011) "In a church, praxis is the constant rhythm that includes study and reflection in continual interaction with engagement and action" (Kindle location, 246). Practice is what you consistently do; praxis is how you consistently improve what you do. There is an inherent humility in praxis; it does not presume to know the best way to operate. Praxis is an attitude of adaptation with a laser focus on the core values.

Practice is not as open to insight or hindsight. In the timber fields of Alaska, lumberjacks were grinding away at their system of safety and productivity, and the team mowed its way through the verdant expanse. In the midst of the buzz and bustle, a new pickup truck pulled up and out stepped one of the company's leaders. The vigor of the task at hand reached its penultimate as workers sought to make a good impression.

This story took place before the invention of GPS, so the leader tucked some topographical maps in his safety harness and climbed to the tallest tree to survey the progress. When he reached the flimsy top, he pulled out his maps and began to observe. Swaying gently back and forth, the foreman triangulated between two landmarks and his location. Then he frantically shouted, "Stop everything! We're in the wrong forest." to which the manager on the ground shouted back, "Keep it down, we are making good progress."

The warning of the foreman was based on new information and a laser focus of the chief objectives of the company. Practice ruthlessly asking, "Is something being done well?" Praxis ruthlessly asks, "Is the right thing being done to the best of our ability?" The manager was more concerned with activity than accomplishment when they responded to the new information. The leader was open to observable indicators that they were, in fact, doing the right thing in the wrong place.

Back to an American missionary in Asia, would you leverage the same strategies that worked in the United States? What would be your agenda the first ten weeks of your tenure? Would you observe the people before you imported your strategy into a culture you did not yet understand? Those who would skip this vital step would have to learn hard, painful lessons about contextualization of the gospel methods in a foreign setting. The message of the gospel must never change, but the methods must change regularly to meet people at the wells of their own culture.

This contextualization is something Jesus intuitively modeled. In John 4, the Bible says, "Jesus knew the Pharisees had heard that he was baptizing and making more disciples than John. So, he left Judea and returned to Galilee. He had to go through Samaria on the way" (*John 4:1,3,4, NLT*). Any Jewish person of Jesus' day would have a great deal of trepidation regarding the statement that Jesus "had to go through Samaria." During this time, a fastidious Jew would never go through Samaria.

During Jesus' day, the previous 500 years proved rocky regarding race relations between the Jewish people and the Samaritan people. It had become so strained that hatred had been built up between the two groups to the extent that the Jews had no dealings with them, and in fact, would not even acknowledge the presence of a Samaritan.

This bigotry and racism would make a Jew travel twice as far to get from Galilee in the North to Judea in the south. That is why I love Jesus. Jesus moves people from racism to "gracism." Do you know why racial reconciliation matters to God? Racial reconciliation matters to God because racial prejudices question the creation of God. The disciples had only been walking with Jesus a short while, and Jesus took them to a place they had been taught since childhood to avoid. If you start walking with Jesus, before long, He will make you confront any prejudices in your heart. John writes,

> Eventually, he came to the Samaritan village of Sychar, near the field that Jacob gave to his son Joseph. Jacob's well was there; and Jesus, tired from the long walk, sat wearily beside the well about noontime. Soon a Samaritan woman came to draw water, and Jesus said to her, "Please give me a drink." He was alone at the time because his disciples had gone into the village to buy some food (*John 4:5-8, NLT*).

As you may know, it was very uncommon for a woman to come to this well alone, at this hour of the day. Culturally and historically, the women of the village would come in the early morning hours to get their day's supply of water. The drawing of water was very much a social thing; it's the modern equivalent of coffee with friends or a yoga class. However, this woman did not fit in with the other women of the society. She was an outcast, because of her adulterous reputation. So, she had to get water alone to dodge the disdain of the women, and she showed up at Jacob's well at noon.

Jacob's well was a couple of thousand years old when Jesus was there and is still functioning today over 4000 years later. The well is in the shadow of Mt. Gerizim. Mt. Gerizim is hallowed to the Samaritans. They do not believe that God dwells in the temple in Jerusalem, but that God dwells on Mt. Gerizim. Jesus said to the woman, "Give me a drink." John recalled, "The woman was surprised, for Jews refuse to have anything to do with Samaritans. She said to Jesus, 'You are a Jew, and I am a Samaritan woman. Why are you asking me for a drink?'" (*John 4:9, NLT*).

Jesus did not answer the woman's question at all. Why? Perhaps the reason is because the enemy keeps people blind through arguing. Jesus did not take the bait to get into a gender or race-based argument. John continues,

> Jesus replied, ``If you only knew the gift God has for you and who you are speaking to, you would ask me, and I would give you living water." "But sir, you don't have a rope or a bucket," she said, "and this well is very deep. Where would you get this living water? And besides, do you think you're greater than our ancestor Jacob, who gave us this well? How can you offer better water than he and his sons and his animals enjoyed? *(John 4:10-12, NLT)*.

Here again, Jesus refused the argument bait. Was Jesus theologically equipped to win the argument? Was Jesus philosophically astute enough to bury her talking points in bombastic rectifications? Of course. Practice would have sought to change her mind; Jesus sought to change her heart by focusing with laser intensity upon her actual needs.

Jesus replied, "Anyone who drinks this water will soon become thirsty again.

But those who drink the water I give will never be thirsty again. It becomes a fresh, bubbling spring within them, giving them eternal life" *(John 4: 13-14, NLT)*. Jesus used her physical thirst to strike up a conversation about her spiritual thirst. This was a woman whose whole life was expressed in the carnal. Her voluptuous and relational feelings were what drove her to a point where she could no longer retrieve water at the routine time. Jesus was in the process of showing her that she didn't need to add something to her life. Jesus did not come to make her life better; He came to give her an entirely new life.

The woman replied,

> Please, sir, the woman said, give me this water! Then I'll never be thirsty again, and I won't have to come here to get water. Go and get your husband, Jesus

told her. I don't have a husband, the woman replied. Jesus said You're right! You don't have a husband. For you have had five husbands, and you aren't even married to the man you're living with now. You certainly spoke the truth! Sir, the woman said, you must be a prophet. So, tell me, why is it that you Jews insist that Jerusalem is the only place of worship, while we Samaritans claim it is here at Mount Gerizim, where our ancestors worshiped? *(John 4:15-20, NLT)*.

She had gone through five husbands looking for one of them to completely satisfy her. There is a God-sized hole in every life; only Jesus perpetually satisfies a human soul. No matter the context, no matter the person, the church has the answer to the problem if we approach people in such a way that we meet their needs. That is the case for every person in every situation, in every culture. Notice how she wanted to argue theologically with Jesus.

Jesus replied,

Believe me, dear woman; the time is coming when it will no longer matter whether you worship the Father on this mountain or in Jerusalem. You Samaritans know very little about the one you worship, while we Jews know all about Him, for salvation comes from the Jews. But the time is coming—indeed it's here now— when true worshipers will worship the Father in spirit and truth. The Father is looking for those who will worship him that way. For God is Spirit, so those who worship Him must worship in spirit and truth. *(John 4:21-24, NLT)*.

Jesus was saying, God, is not confined to this Mountain. God is not limited to Jerusalem. God is a Spirit. He is everywhere. You can't capture Him and put Him in your little box. He is a Spirit, and as such He must be worshiped in Spirit, and in truth. The woman said, "I know the Messiah is coming—the One who is called Christ. When He comes, He will explain everything to us." Here again, you can see the master manipulator; she completely disregarded the profound things Jesus just said and tried to kick the can of the conversation because she didn't want to deal with her condition. Her reaction was standard operating procedure for those far from God in any culture.

> Then Jesus told her, I am the Messiah! Just then His disciples came back. They were shocked to find him talking to a woman, but none of them had the nerve to ask, what do you want with her? or Why are you talking to her? The woman left her water jar beside the well and ran back to the village, telling everyone, Come and see a man who told me everything I ever did! Could he possibly be the Messiah? So, the people came streaming from the village to see Him. (*John 4:26-30, NLT*).

Jesus modeled the missional methodology with this interaction. Jesus knew He was the answer but saw the individual through the lens of her needs, and then Socratically brought her to the realization of who he was through her own felt need. It is important to note; John the Baptist declared Jesus was the Messiah, by this time, many of the disciples stated Jesus was the Messiah. However, this was the first time Jesus said, "I am the Messiah." That is an essential piece of information; because of to whom, Jesus revealed His identity.

She did not represent the religious elite in Jerusalem; she did not even represent the religious elite in Samaria. Instead, she represented the outcast of the outcast, the marginalized of the marginalized. Jesus chose her to be the first person to whom He would personally declare who he was.

Jesus abolished this racial divide and set the full narrative up for the gospel. If you remember, in Acts, before Jesus was taken into Heaven after His resurrection, He told the disciples to go to Jerusalem and wait for the outpouring of the Holy Spirit. Then he said, "After you are baptized with the Holy

Spirit then you would be My witnesses in Jerusalem, in Judea, in Samaria and to the ends of the earth" (*Acts 1:8, NLT*).

When the woman said, "Come and see a man who told me everything I ever did." What was she saying? She was saying see a man who told me everything I ever did and yet loved me anyway. Jesus modeled the path to reach our communities no matter the given context. We must be willing to lay aside all of our preconceived notions about who we are supposed to reach and how we are supposed to reach them and identify a real need. The missional ministry is praxis in nature; it is continually asking contextual questions.

Contextual questions are not to water down the message. Note, Jesus did not avoid talking about sin; He instead revealed God's shocking love for the sinner. Among the shocked in this narrative were the disciples. Their practice told them they were not supposed to even be there. Their practice told them that Jesus should not be talking to a woman alone, especially this woman. However, Jesus modeled missional ministry to the surprise of the disciples, and as a result, an entire city was reached for Jesus.

Branson and Martinez (2011) state, "Missional formation refers to how God shapes a church to participate in God's love for the world" (Kindle location, 650). Missional formation receives insight from the church's context, as well as biblically informed values from the church's cortex. This praxis forces a collision of what Argyris and Schon (1974) juxtaposed as "Theory-in-use versus Espoused theory." The Espoused Theory is what people believe their values are, based on their motives and models.

Theory-in-use is the reality of which a person is that results from behavioral systems that are often latent. In other words, often the church espouses to be a church that is for everyone no matter his or her race, financial wherewithal, education, or religious background (Espoused Theory) yet our behavior is exclusive from the outsider, underprivileged, and undereducated (Theory-in-use).

Understanding that there is a gap between our desired intentions and our behavior is the first step in systems thinking that reshapes our praxis. It is the organizational equivalent of looking in the mirror. Have you ever seen someone out in public and just had the passing thought, *I'm not sure if they saw a mirror?* His or her hair is matted in an I slept awesome last night pattern, the stained shirt they don can identify their breakfast menu, and yet their confidence is off the charts. The false tattered yet confident individual in many ways is like some churches. We confidently walk through the world, and erroneously think *don't you want to be just like me?*

If a church is not receiving feedback from strategic mirrors placed throughout the organization, then the church can look just as ridiculous as a messy person without a mirror perspective. The Church says it is all about evangelism, yet what measurable way is the Church training and leading the church to do evangelism in its context? When was the last time the church looked in a Theory-in-use mirror to see if they had a practice or praxis?

The Attractional Model

When COVID hit in March of 2020 we had one online service and I held an emergency board meeting that night. I showed them a picture of our morning broadcast quality with 18-year-old TV cameras side by side to a picture from the News. I said, "this is what everyone is comparing us to when they watch our online service." The board overwhelmingly voted to purchase 4K equipment. While not every church is able to go out and immediately upgrade their quality, a commitment to excellence whether you were attracting people online or in-person is a marathon not a sprint. This commitment to excellence must be engaged every week from here forward. It took us time but by being urgently intentional, and brutally honest we have been able to catapult our online experience well beyond the standard.

I have heard pastors erroneously say, "We just did online for quarantine, I'm glad that's over." Well, saying online is "offer" is tantamount to Sears saying, "Amazon is just a trend." The post-COVID church must assess the attractional elements online, now more than ever. When we first launched our YouTube channel the average watch time was three minutes. However, we kept improving our video and music quality every week. In 2021 our YouTube channel was watched over 63,000 hours. In the first five months of 2022 our YouTube channel has been watched over 88,000 hours. The biggest crowd you will speak to every week in your online crowd.

Three Big Sundays

Momentum has taken hit after hit during COVID. One way to begin to gain momentum is to plan out three to four big Sundays in a row. We do this around times that people are naturally interested in church, Christmas, Easter, and September. Christmas and Easter are obvious, and September is a when month people who have been out of church start to look for a church because they have got their kids back into a routine of school.

Identify the weeks you want to make big. Next evaluate your resources. Can you produce an illustrated sermon? Can you bring in a Christian Artist? At City Church we started doing a Blessing of the Bikes in the spring and a car show in the fall. At the first Blessing of the Bikes we had over 50 bikers show up, we had bikes on stage, and I preached in my Harley shirt an illustrated sermon called Life is a Highway, which the band covered.

The car show we called Cruise with a Cause, and the church matched the $30.00 registration fee and 100% of the money raised went for cleft palate surgeries in India. The cars arrived an hour before service, I preached an illustrated message about cars, then we had food and an audience judging after the service.

These ideas may not work for you, but the question is, what resources do you have. God will always give you a jar with oil in it, or a red cord you can throw out of a window, or an old wooden staff you can throw down. What do you have in your hand?

12-Month Missional/ Attractional Calendar

When a bone is broken, the doctors will place a cast on it. The cast serves as a guide for growth. It protects the vulnerable spot in the body until the body can strengthen the weak spot. The body has a miraculous ability to heal itself if given the opportunity. The church is the same way. When something is broken, it needs to be put in a cast to protect the vulnerable place until the body heals.

The Post-COVID Church suggests a 12-month missional and attractional calendar to serve as a cast or a brace until the vulnerability is no longer a liability. The body of Christ will heal itself if given the right conditions and protections with which to do it. This cast is not intended to fix your practice, but rather to inform your praxis. The cast will also teach your team how to continually contextualize your methodology to meet the needs of your community. The cast will elicit engagement from every system of the church, as a missional mindset is set. In the case of a broken bone, having to set the bone is the most painful part of the recovery. Such is the case for this transition. Pain in the church context occurs when something broken has grown together, and it must be broken again before it can be adequately healed.

Once you have your three big Sundays on the calendar focused on natural times of church growth, next you fill in the gaps with emphasis upon the church's missional strategy. In the church setting, there must be an inward focus that is repaired. When the eyes of the church are inward, vision is impaired to a nearsighted perspective. Nearsightedness, or Myopia, is when the light is not focused properly coming into the retina, resulting in the inability to see far away clearly. To repair the impaired vision, a lens is required to force the eye to focus the light properly (Heiting, 2014). The same is true with church vision. Scripture states of the church, "You are the light of the world" (*Matthew 5:14, NLT*). When the light is not properly focused, it creates a blurred perspective of the vision, resulting in the ability only to see clearly the things that are close.

Nearsightedness in the church's vision is synonymous with an inward focus. The burden for the lost is overridden by the inability to properly focus the light to see that the fields are "ripe for harvest." Jesus challenged His followers saying, "You know the saying, 'Four months between planting and harvest.' But I say, wake up and look around. The fields are already ripe for harvest" (*John 4:35, NLT*). Jesus was utilizing an agrarian analogy that all of His hearers understood. After the planting time, many sat back and took an inward focus on the fields.

Jesus' call to "Wake up and look around" was a clear message to the posture of the spiritual climate of His time, and even more so the time in which we live. Wake up denotes the church has overslept and has hit the snooze button one too many times. When a body is asleep, it shuts down its functions to the minimum needed to stay alive to recover through rest. Likewise, when the body of Christ is sleeping, the body is not functioning at the level needed to do what the church is called to do. Therefore, the church needs to heed the warning of our Lord to wake up and look around.

Look Around

Jesus' charge to His disciples was to "look around." Look around; what do you see as you look around your community? Look around; what are the needs that are visible outside of the walls of the church? Look at what gifts the church has to offer. Look around; how can the church leverage its greatest gifts to meet the community's greatest needs?

Genuine life change and church growth take place when the greatest gifts of the church intersect with the greatest needs of the community. The convergence of the unmet needs of the community with the God-empowered gifts for the community result in the church's purpose being fulfilled, the Kingdom of God expanding, and the church growing. Knowing what you know now about your current city if you were to start all over again, where would you start? It is easy to feel stuck in our present condition because ministerial myopia has slowly changed the focus of light.

So, imagine for a moment that you are not in your current position, but instead, you are consulting for the person coming in to lead the church forward. What would you tell them are the greatest needs of the community? Many times, a fresh perspective comes from new information. If you do not seek community information outside of your sphere of influence, then you will only make cyclical conclusions. These are conclusions that end up with the same results because there is no new information. A church in this phase needs a linear change to arrive at a fresh conclusion. A linear change in a church is when the body of Christ receives new information that is derived from the needs of the community, which aligns with the gifts of the church.

Linear changes in business take place when a new product or service reshapes the industry in which it serves. For the church, strategic linear change is when the laser focus of the church intersects with the gaping needs of the community. Focusing the light on those who are far from God and leveraging the gifts of the church to meet those needs creates an outward vision.

Start with the need. When creating strategic linear change and an outward vision, the church must first identify the greatest need that requires new information. It is likely that if a committee or church member who has been serving the Lord a long time identifies the needs, they will have a skewed perspective. This defective approach is often seen in short-term mission ventures across the world.

Imagine if a church from the United States travels to a foreign country thinking it is going to reach those in a developing nation by doing a marriage conference for those over 40. Once they are on the ground, they find out that the average age is 16 as a result of a pandemic, so they need to focus on children's ministry. Information that is in a bubble will not identify actual needs. While the church coming from America had a great heart to help people with marriages, their information was derived from the bubble in which they live. The church from America would be answering a question the church in Sub-Saharan Africa is not asking.

This same type of cultural overreach is often used when a church attempts to reach out to its community. When it inevitably does not work, the church feels like a failure and writes off these types of efforts with a dismissive, "We tried outreach, and it just does not work." To do real missions work inside the community the church must ask questions about what needs are greatest in the community, and once that information is fully understood, then ask *how I can adapt my methods to equip those in my church better to reach those in their lives?* Missional questions start with missional understanding.

What is the growing demographic around the church property? Are there a plethora of young families moving into the area? Are families of different ethnicities moving in around you? Problems arise in a church's mission when she ceases to look like her community. The same is true for the average age, as well as ethnic and financial diversity. Does your church consist of people of means, while people who lack means are moving into the neighborhood? What are the gaps between the community and the church?

You will succeed in refocusing your church if you mind the gaps. If you mind the gaps, the margins will grow. Think deeply and broadly about the existing gaps between the way your church and community differ. In minding the gap, you are doing the same thing Jesus did when He kicked off a conversation with the woman at the well. There was a great gap between the two theologically, culturally, and racially. However, Jesus modeled what He instructed the church to do, and that is look up. As Jesus looked up from His needs, He saw her needs. Remember, at the time, Jesus was quite thirsty. However, Jesus insisted on talking to the woman about her unquenchable thirst. Jesus minded the gap, and in doing so reached a city.

It is possible that you will not get fresh information about your city's needs from within the Christian bubble of your church leaders. One way to begin to get a new perspective is to search your city's data on the Internet. Every year more and more vital information about cities' demographics compile to these types of databases. Information regarding medium age, ethnic groups that are growing, average education levels, crime rates, and so much more can be found in one place.

If your church does not look like your community, you are going to need to pull people into the conversation that can provide a holistic picture of your community. One way to do this is to invite the teachers of the year from each school to a nice meal. In doing this not only can you honor those who are working hard in the community, but there is also no greater assemblage of people who can relate the needs and changes within a community like a star teacher. They are teachers of the year because they care about their students. This love drives them to go way beyond the call of duty, and it is that passion that the church needs to harness.

This nice meal for the teachers should only have one request at the end; for them to fill out a survey identifying the greatest needs of the community. This empirical information, along with the data from the city, should be compared to the church's greatest gifts. When the church focuses its light on the need, then strategic linear change will begin to take place.

What are your gifts? To answer this query, you may need to ask questions like: *When people think about our church what comes to mind? What are we best at doing? When people think about our church, do they think about music, drama, youth ministry?* After you identify your greatest gifts, then align those gifts with the information you gather about your community. For example, if many of your star teachers identified a lack of creative art outlets in the community, and your church is best known for musicals or other art-related elements, then the convergence of needs and gifts will produce strategic linear change. Needs in a community are as diverse as the gifts in a church; therefore, you need to customize your 12-month missional calendar with the full knowledge of your greatest gifts and the community's greatest need.

The Twelve-Month Calendar

This calendar is a cast to fix what may be broken or needs to be strengthened. The calendar is a corrective lens to allow the church to begin to correct any nearsightedness. Because of that, there needs to be holistic embracing of this church-wide focus. Resist calling it a campaign. The terminology around campaign words has short-term parameters. The vision has to start at the top. Buy-in for the missional calendar must percolate from the pastor to the pew. Therefore, sermon planning must be intentional and strategic for this 12-month period.

Preach to reach. Plan 12 evangelistic services a year. While every church service should have an offer to pray with those who need to accept Christ, there needs to be intentional-planning and vision casting that goes into the 12 reach days. These monthly staples should engage all of the strengths of the church into a well thought out weekend worship experience that leverages your gifts while engaging the lost. The week before these reach days the pastor will dedicate his or her message to the church being empowered to fulfill its mission. Throughout those messages, the pastor will be ramping up the vision for the reach days.

These ramp weeks will be focused on centering the light of the church on the Great Commission. The ramp weeks should include testimonies of life change and salvation along with highlighting how one invitation to church can make a difference. This is where the attractional intersects with the missional. There has to be a change in thinking, perspective, as well as actions to see a strategic linear change in the church. Therefore, a hybrid of the two models is necessary to see substantive post-COVID growth.

For the reach week, you should leverage creative people. You may call this a creative team. A creative team is simply a group of innovators who think out of the box and have the passion and skill set to execute ideas that would set that weekend apart and raise the level. It has been said that none of us are as smart as all of us. Therefore, build a team of people with the express purpose of prioritizing the Great Commission in these key services. Part of the role of these creative people is to cause the visitor to encounter the Bible through layers, as well as give the people in the church memorable elements to talk about the next day at work.

Once my church rented a large petting zoo to help illustrate Noah's Ark. We had the animals' parade in by entering a set that resembled the ark, which was just a door leading to the outside. There were zebras, kangaroos, a Bearcat, a giant Burmese python, and the list goes on. Then the door to the ark was closed, and a storm took place inside the church. Giant industrial fans kicked on, strobe lights flashed, and people sprayed mist water into the air to give it that extra touch. While clearly, that takes work, the town was buzzing the next day, and it was one of our largest crowds and greatest altar calls.

Noah's Ark was not the first stab at a creative weekend, so begin by working with what you have; think about your context, leverage your gifts, and see what God will do. There was another weekend that had a Back to the Future theme. There was a nice man that let us drive his DeLorean into the sanctuary. This may not be your style, and that's okay. The goal is to leverage what is at your disposal to help tell the greatest story of all.

In addition to creating reach weeks and ramps weeks, to each of them, next, you need to plan 24 missions. In the context of understanding your community's needs and utilizing your church's gifts, plan 24 activities that get the church out of the church building. These could range from serving at a soup kitchen to handing out ice-cold bottles of water with the church's name on them at the Fourth of July fireworks. The goal is to get the eyes of the church focused on things that are farther away. Times of serving will not only build a heart for evangelism and underscore the purpose of the church, but it will bond people together as they serve arm in arm. The bond that takes place when people are serving a need is greater than the bond from staring at the back of someone's head in a service for two months.

When All Else Fails, Cancel Service

One way to show the value of the missional mindset of the church was we canceled service the weekend of Labor Day. We had shirts for everyone. Our first teams were serving the homeless at 6:30 AM in downtown Memphis. Then everyone met at the church for a rally, coffee, and donuts, and went out into the community to give away free cold bottles of water with the church's logo, and a scan code that took them to a three-minute message from me inviting them to the next three weeks at City. Memphis has the largest urban park in America. We sent teams of people with 2000 cold bottles of water to invite people who were at the park to visit our church. The people in the park were shocked to hear that we canceled service just to meet them.

Prioritize the Church's Priorities

Twenty-four well-placed opportunities will create many stories that must be leveraged. Find someone with a cell phone and a little video experience. Have them record a one-minute testimony of those who are serving. The video should include how serving in the community has made them think differently and why they want to come again and serve. Just as important as touching the lives of those with whom you are serving, are the stories of those who are doing the serving. It is their stories that will begin to dislodge stuck ways of thinking and begin to soften hardened hearts toward the lost.

You can guarantee that there will be some critics. There are people whose motto is, "I shall not be, I shall not be moved." Understand two things. These people are not enemies of you or enemies of the lost. Most are simply enemies of change. Often, if you just give them an outlet with which to listen to them, continue to preach biblical messages about reaching the lost, and show them the stories of changed lives, many of them will come around.

A few of them never will come around, and that is okay too. You might ask, *but what if the resistant people are the pillars of the church?* All pillars do is hold things up. You as a leadership team must preach the Gospel of Jesus, and occasionally that means letting the human-made pillars fall. Our job is obedience.

In addition to the reach and ramp weeks and the 24 mission events, work the message of the "why", the "what", and the "how" of the church into your discipleship systems as well, albeit Sunday school, or small groups. Choose a curriculum that allows for an underlying of the core values, chief objectives, and strategies of the church to be underscored over and over again.

Understand the Calendar Dos and Don'ts.

Do check the scheduled events against the regional and school calendars. A great way to bleed momentum is to pour time, money, and effort into an outreach event only for it to be swamped by a litany of preexisting commitments. Notes should be placed on the church calendar regarding long weekends for school, prom, homecoming, as well as spring, and fall breaks. Additionally, seasonal, and regional notes, based on your context. I am from the South, so among things to consider is the opening of hunting season, certain football rivalry games, as well as the opening of NASCAR season at the Daytona 500.

You can idealistically plan events on top of these major conflicts of schedule, or you can perspicaciously not compete with deeply embedded cultural and social structure. Momentum is most costly in the early stages of development. Therefore, you should be cautious about setting your calendar to compete.

Don't create the calendar in isolation. As your leadership team endeavors to broaden the missional approach of your church, you should identify all the necessary people to execute the desired plans and in advance and bring them into a vision casting and planning meeting. Although you may feel you know how you want to proceed, the goal of this stage is onboarding the essential people. If people feel inclusion, they will be part of the solution.

Don't neglect training and discipleship opportunities on your missional calendar. Part of the goal of being missional is empowering the church to do the work of the ministry. Therefore, you develop creative ways to engage people in training. As church leaders, we want people to share their faith. However, how many training opportunities do we provide to help them win in this and other areas? These training times should be strategically preached about in the lead up to the opportunities. If the pastor knows there is a training session coming up, he or she should teach the biblical antecedent for that commission in the lead-up to that sign-up.

Finally, do envelop your calendar in prayer. Solomon penned, "We can make our plans,

but the Lord determines our steps." (*Proverbs 16:9, NLT*). Your team can accomplish a lot after you pray, but they can accomplish very little effectively before you pray. If you have an existing prayer team, task them with covering the events of the calendar in prayer. Prayer is the ultimate momentum builder; it moves mountains, and it can indeed move your church.

Conclusion

Learn to change the pattern of the way you approach systems thinking. Don't be like the WHO, who broke an entire ecosystem through unintended consequences. To solve a problem, don't create three more. Learn to see with that new perspective so hindsight and insight can inform your strategic change. Through the use of double-loop learning, you, as a church, can isolate the causality of the real issues and adjust your strategy and change your structure.

Both attractional and missional models must be employed to grow and to gain momentum. The missional calendar will serve as a cast as well as corrective lenses to repair ministry myopia. Once the light of the church is properly focused on the retina of missional development, then a fresh and clear vision for those far from God will come into focus.

The 12-month calendar will not be an end, but a means to develop a heart for those far from God within your community. The calendar is all about sowing and reaping. If you sow more seeds into your community, the church will grow.

You will grow in direct proportion to the seed you sow.

The missional and attractional calendar is an intentional way to structure sowing, so you have harvest coming in at every possible point. One of the most critical elements is the need to tell the stories of changed lives. As priorities shift, it is imperative to remind those who may question why the priorities are shifting. The curation of these redemptive stories is one of the most powerful corrective lenses a church can apply. When we see lives truly changed by Jesus, then we will not mind a little change for Jesus.

Chapter Five

Objectively Revisit Your Church Culture

Your church culture is the combination of what you unintentionally tolerate and intentionally develop.

Culture is the embedded behavioral norms and ways of processing and prioritizing information, resources, and focus. Culture is the overarching pattern through which all thoughts and actions are managed, albeit intentional or unintentional. The greatest sermons in the world can be either implemented by a church culture or rejected by a church culture. The best strategies in the world can be leveraged or limited by an existing church culture. The best strategic plan will never survive an entrenched negative culture. Chand (2011) said it best, "Culture eats strategy for lunch. You can have a good strategy in place, but if you don't have the culture and the enabling systems, the negative culture of the organization will defeat the strategy" (Kindle location, 201).

If a church culture is healthy, even poorly conceived plans can succeed. Conversely, if a church has an unhealthy culture, even the best strategic plans can fall impotent to implementation. What defines healthy and unhealthy cultures is the ability to receive, process, and implement a strategy in such a way that it drives the organization toward its goals without compromising its values.

The first element of a healthy church culture is its ability to receive strategy. Strategy receptors are related to an organization's willingness to acknowledge that specific behaviors attributes which contribute to certain results. The greatest enemy of strategy receptors is the knee-jerk reaction to give an excuse.

*Excuses will lull a group into an organizational rigor
mortis that stiffens the muscular system by refusing and
redefining vital information.*

George Washington Carver said, "99 % of all failures come
from people who have a habit of making excuses" (Kremer,
1991). The brilliance of this botanist and inventor extends far
beyond the scale and scope of the agricultural world; Carver
understood systems. When a pattern of excuse-making per-
vades a culture, it will throw the entire organization into a state
of resisting constructive input. Once the excuses are no longer
part of the pattern, and then growth can emerge in the form of
welcomed accountability.

Another reason an organization will not receive strategy is a
fear of change. Ironically people are more afraid of failure than
they are of dying (Merdrano, 2011). It is up to leaders in the
organization to take a good look at those who would be most
resistant to needed change, and through a collaborative conversation, implement a way to process strategy where all the
leaders of the church arrive at a shared conclusion.

The church must be more afraid of death than change.

One definition of death is "ceasing to change." In the human
body, death happens when there is a cessation of circular,
respiratory systems, and brain activity. When the body stops
changing it is dead. Change is the only thing that keeps a body
alive.

The same is true of the body of Christ. We begin to die spiritually
when our body stops becoming like Jesus. The influence of the
church begins to die when we refuse to augment or nuance our
methodology to accomplish our missiology.

Resistance to all change takes place when a body of Christ is
more concerned with comfort than competence. Fear of failure is
associated with a fear of change. However, in an ironic twist, the
failure to change is the most frequent predecessor to failure. Fear
immobilizes us; it makes us think we can't move. Fear lies to us,
saying "The safest course of action is inaction." Nevertheless,
inaction is still an action and indecision is still a decision.

The second aspect of an organization having a healthy culture is its ability to process strategy. A process is a series of steps or actions taken which yield the same desired result. Workers at all levels of the organization must have the functional wherewithal to see a strategy from stage to stage as they envision the desired outcome.

It is imperative to note the difference between a process and a cycle. A process is one, two, three, and four. A cycle is one, two, three, and one.

An unhealthy organization will put strategies through a cycle, ultimately starting over at one, all the while thinking they are going through a process. This trait is especially dominant in a church culture that struggles to decide. A process moves strategies through clearly defined stages, resulting in the capacity to implement.

The third element of a healthy culture is the ability to implement the strategy. Whereas processing strategy is about attitude, implementing strategy is about aptitude. Implementing strategy is the operational capacity to integrate the elements derived from the processes into the behavioral fabric of the organization.

Implementation is when strategy translates into habitual and accountable patterns of behavior. Once this strategy is part of the normative behavior, it must also take priority in the hiring and training process. Schultz & Yang (2014) note, "Whatever your culture, your values, your guiding principles, you have to take steps to inculcate them in the organization early in its life so that they can guide every decision, every hire, every strategic objective you set" (p.81).

For Shultz, executive chairman of Starbucks, his implementtation of the strategy is on display for all to experience. Shultz stated, "We are not in the coffee business serving people; we are in the people business serving coffee." (Michelli, p.28). The implementation of this core value is seen every time the barista calls you by name. Many well-crafted strategies have imploded inside the cogs of receiving, processing, and implementing the stated strategies.

This functional capability must be empowered with a purpose-filled intrinsic drive to meet the stated objective. You have to want change before you can "will" change. It is up to the leader to develop the vision to such a clear stage that people want to be part of the shared outcome. Conversely, if the leader cannot communicate the vision of the strategy in a contagious and clear way, then it will take more time and resources to move the strategy forward. If you are a leader who is passionate about the needed change, but just not a strong communicator of vision, be honest enough to get some coaching in that area. Your modeling a desire for growth personally will drive those on your team to do the same.

The culture within your church dictates the behaviors and motivations of your ministry functions. Schein (2010) states, "Culture is to a group what personality or character is to an individual" (p. 14). Have you ever been with someone with an unhealthy personality? If given the option, we don't want to be around these people very long. You may minister to them, but you certainly do not invite them on vacation. If given a choice, we would not work with them. The same is true for the personality of a church. If the culture is not a healthy one, then it does not inspire new people to want to gravitate toward the vision. Chand (2011) notes, "When the difficulty revolves around people, it's probably a culture problem that won't be solved by any strategy or vision. The only solution is to change the culture." (Kindle location, 633).

Many times, churches say they want fresh vision, and they may even be seeking a new strategy. However, the cultural maladies that got them to the place where they are struggling must be squarely addressed before any strategy or vision has a chance at succeeding. Unintentional or intentional, there are sabotaging mechanisms embedded within negative cultural constructs that have the power to remove the impetus for any well-crafted initiative. Therefore, it is up to the leadership team to unify the heart of their influencers toward deriving a strategy that is embraced and owned by all.

Chand (2011) notes, "Culture problems, by their very nature are never solved quickly. They require a clear understanding of the problem, a commitment to systematic change, and persistence to see change take root." (Kindle location, 385). It must be acknowledged that the organizational DNA did not get to its current place overnight, and the elements that need to change will not take place overnight. The cultural correction is a journey. During this part of the refocusing process, group analysis of the existing culture within the church is time well spent by the leadership team. If a leader does not manage his or her culture, their culture will manage them. Begin identifying the culture by having a dialogue about outcomes without ascribing blame to individuals.

After surgery, I had to go to months of physical therapy. Therapy is not fun. You are given a seemingly menial task, yet it brings agony. It is a one-two punch to the ego and the body. I will never forget the first time the therapist walked me to a flight of stairs. Fear overtook me just looking at the task ahead.

Previous to this surgery I had been skydiving multiple times. The last jump was at 18,500 feet. But now, seven feet down to a landing was enough to paralyze my mind with fear. I remember looking multiple times at the therapist as if to say, are you sure I can do this? Finally, the therapist said, "you can do it." It is humbling to be 38 years old and afraid to start going downstairs.

Organizations that are stuck naturally react the same way to this type of cultural work. We are afraid it is going to hurt. I should have been more afraid to stay on a walker than I was to switch to a cane. I should have been more scared of not being able to navigate stairs than I was taking one step.

The pain had been so great, that it reframed my risk analysis.

That is what happens with churches that are struggling. The

pain of struggling to grow becomes so real that it reframes our risk analysis. We become immobilized with fear; fear of failure, fear of pain, and fear of being uncomfortable.

One thing I had to give up when I started therapy was being afraid to be uncomfortable. Everything about therapy was uncomfortable. Yet, I had a choice, did I want to be whole, or did I want to be broken? Did I want to be uncomfortable for a little while so I could be comfortable for life? Yes, there is fear of change. However, just like my fear was mitigated by the confident, "you can do it," coming from the therapist, your fear can be assuaged by the Holy Spirit's voice. He has led you to read this book and to have these conversations. So, let's take the next step. You can do it!

Cultural Profile

Ask the following questions in a team setting:

What successes do we celebrate the most?

Who are our heroes?

What churches do we aspire to be like in style and substance?

What ministries inspire us to become greater?

Why do we exist?

What is the purpose of our church in our town?

If Jesus became our pastor, what would He do to move us forward?

Perhaps more importantly, what would Jesus stop doing if He led our church?

What would Jesus want to change regarding our church's approach to the community?

What would Jesus be excited about in our ministry?

If I were not saved, what would draw me to, or push me away from our church?

If money were not an issue, what would we change about our church?

What are our non-negotiable values?

What is our greatest threat?

Where is our greatest opportunity to grow?

What is most likely to happen if we fail to change?

As you navigate through these questions, a profile of your culture will emerge. The gap between who you are and who you desire to become must be organized into clearly defined stages of a process. For my therapy, I had a goal to get home. I was living full time at the rehab center for the days following the surgery. I was unable to go home because I had to climb a flight of stairs to get to the main floor of my house, and another flight to get to my master bedroom. If I could not climb stairs, I could not go home. So, the gap between where I was and where I needed to be was the ability to navigate stairs. I had to set daily goals related to climbing stairs. The good news about fear is that it is conquerable. Albeit the fear of stairs or the fear of change; we should never let fear keep us from being where we want to be and becoming who God wants us to be.

So, what is the gap between where you are and where you need to be? Filling that gap is your objective. The way you accomplish that objective is your strategy. While in rehab once I became able to take one step my strategy was to take one more step every day until I could navigate an entire flight. Ignoring fears of pain or change will never get you back to health. It is incumbent upon you to lead your team through incremental steps of climbing to the next level.

Team Up

Making strategy is a team sport. The same elements required to build a great sporting team is required to develop a strategy. It takes talent, it takes planning, it takes collaboration, and it takes engagement. Ackermann and Eden (2011) note, "Strategy derives from the thinking, conversations, and negotiated agreements within groups" (p. 417)

Team thinking is essential for organizational commitment. Not only does it engage a variety of resources, backgrounds, and experiences, but also it engages the people behind those resources. Group thinking moves people from the armchair critic to the passionate enthusiast. Ackermann and Eden (2011) state, we must, "...achieve emotional and thinking (cognitive) commitment as it drives the process of making strategy" (p.614). Group thinking engages people and gives them ownership.

Making strategy can be a unifying process by building community, identity, and organizational commitment in the church. Ackermann and Eden articulate a few action steps that must be considered, "Start where each participant is at, his or her immediate and personal role concerns." Beginning with immediate and individual concerns is central to moving the process forward. Personal concerns are sometimes rational and other times irrational. However, those at the functional levels of the team will never be able to see solutions until they have had the opportunity to express these concerns. Many at the executive level have already processed through a series of information and options, and often they do this without the whole perspective of everyone on the team. Additionally, some of the most brilliant solutions come from those at the operational level.

Next, Ackermann and Eden (2011) state, "Seek to develop new options rather than fighting old ones" (p.614). If you have been working with your team awhile, you may be able to forecast the responses of some to new initiatives. However, coaching your team in advance to this phase is critical. Team thinking, team conversations, and team negotiation exercises are just some of the ways to create fully engaged people, assimilate the best ideas, and stimulate long-term organizational commitment. With it, challenges become doable, and victory becomes achievable. Without, coaching beforehand it is leadership equivalent of pushing a stone uphill; it can be done, but momentum will not be on your side and the ones pushing get tired quickly.

How do you allow engagement without letting the loud voices in the organization dominate the future objectives? Some people in a team get their way through volume. Understanding this notion to manipulate is the reason the leader must get everyone to agree on the shared values. Once the values are agreed upon, as you begin to talk through the shared objecttives, some may push back. At this point in the conversation, the leader must reference the shared values. For instance, we all agree, the church youth ministry needs to attack more middle schoolers. By reminding the team of the shared values, it defuses the ability of one person to verbally bulldoze over an objective that is based upon the value.

In the world of change management, consultants are often sought to navigate the tricky waters of transitioning an organization from self-protecting, mediocre consumers into an operational cog of change. Much of the time consultants are brought in to provide fresh insight and perspective as many in the organization are too intimately involved with the frozen behavior to see a clear non-political or emotional way out of the state of being stuck.

With concerns expressed and a discipline of filtering everything through the grid of shared values, the church is in a state of readiness for strategic change. Weiner (2009) defines it this way, "Readiness as a shared psychological state in which organizational members feel committed to implementing an organizational change and confidence in their collective abilities to do so" (p.6). Value solidification is the glue that holds the stressed organization together during times of shifting objectives and strategies.

Ackermann and Eden (2011) state, "Strategy is about agreeing on priorities and then implementing those priorities toward the realization of organizational purpose" (p.5).

Once the leaders understand the baseline expectations along with the organizational goals, then he or she can lead a strategic shift. Davila (2006) distinguishes three levels of change, "incremental, semi-radical, and radical" (Kindle location, 1325). While incrementalism is the best approach to lasting change, there is palatability for the other two categories of change at different lifecycles in the church. Palatability of change is not a static condition. An organization can be led to embrace greater increments of change through dynamic interaction with values, objectives, and the reality of the church's actual condition.

Burke (2015) notes, "Three criteria for change are (1) valid and useful information, (2) free choice, and (3) internal commitment" (p.186). The framework for culture reconstruction implores these three elements. When it comes to your church, do you have the most valid and useful information? Churches that fail to ask, "what does this information mean?" questions about its data will improperly navigate threats and opportunities that surround them. Information may be valid, but its usefulness is subject to the knowledge of the one receiving the information.

Imagine you had never flown in an airplane, and on your first flight, you were invited to sit in the co-pilot's seat. At that point, you have access to valid information; however, if you do not understand what the information means or how to interpret the information, then the correct information is not useful. Likewise, some in the church leadership team may need to be taught how to use instruments in the cockpit. Information first is correct, and then it is useful.

Free choice is essential to engagement. Pink (2009) argued, "Human beings have an innate inner drive to be autonomous, self-determined, and connected to one another. And when that drive is liberated, people achieve more and live richer lives" (Kindle location, 958). When you tap into the intrinsic part of an individual, you unleash his or her natural potential instead of quenching it for control. The free choice phase is where many leaders get stuck. It is more than appropriate to get a third party such as a consultant to navigate through this phase. Vision is the key, and the ability to communicate that vision is what infuses the desire for engagement in the new processes.

Useful information and engaging free will induce an internal commitment. This commitment cannot be coerced for the result of manipulation but only takes place when the common goal aligns with the internal compass of the team member. Inner commitment is required to endure the changes ahead.

What is the difference between January second at the gym and January 22nd? Internal commitment. This phase of change is where productive habits are formed, and initiatives become internalized to be part of the behavioral fabric.

Conclusion

Culture is key. You can change a lot by changing your culture. Likewise, the best strategies in the world cannot stand up to an entrenched negative culture. Cultural health can empower any organization to crash through the quitting points of change. What defines healthy and unhealthy culture is the ability to *receive, process, and implement* a strategy in such a way that it drives the organization toward its goals without compromising its values. If the values are compromised, then mission drift will change the personality of your church until it is incompatible with the Gospel and impotent to the community. Why we do what we do is drastically more vital than how we do what we do.

Values drive our "why" objectives drive our "what" and strategies drive our "how."

Churches that are unable to receive, process, and implement strategy are doomed to the typical life cycle of a declining organization. The trajectory is fatal and organizational rigor mortis will set in unless significant changes are made in the way the church views its current and future positions. From a spiritual perspective, the ability for a church to receive, process, and implement strategy embodies Jesus' direction to the disciples.

Jesus stated, "I am sending you out like sheep among wolves. Therefore, be as shrewd as snakes and as innocent as doves." *(Mark 10:16, NIV)*. Sheep by nature are not strategic. They have to be protected, led, and fed. However, Jesus' "therefore" was a conjunctive adverb separating the problem from the directive solution. Because you are like sheep headed toward the wolves, be as shrewd as snakes and as innocent as doves. Shrewd in the Greek is *phronimoi*. Shrewdness means, "practically wise, sensible." The clear inference from Jesus is without *phronimoi*, the wolves will devour you, and with *phronimoi*, you can be both effective in your mission and innocent in your message.

The ability to receive, process, and implement strategy is the *phronimoi* of the church. Often, people who refuse constructive change want to take a spiritual stance to ward off change. However, this wholesale resistance to change is the single contributor to church deaths in America. Like sheep, we must maintain a purity of message, but a plasticity of methods. We must allow shrewdness into our missiology that drives us to be more resistant to the wolves, but effective to the lost sheep.

By understanding our existing culture, we see blind spots that keep us in a cyclical pattern and conceive new avenues to grow internally and externally. As we team up, we can evoke a fresh internal commitment to the long-term growth of the church. Remember a bad chapter does not have to be the final chapter. God is still writing your story, and he has mighty things set aside for you and the future of your church.

Chapter Six

Create a Fresh Look

The next phase of the Refocus process is to create a fresh look. This stage is for external recognition, and internal reengagement. COVID caused people to disengage from certain activities they perceived were "non-essential". When many in our consumerist culture placed church attendance in the "non-essential" category they removed the rhythm of worship from their schedules, their lives, and their hearts. This step is vital, but it is not exclusively focused on the people you lost but rather the lost in general.

The next time you visit the grocery store take note of how many items brandish the words "new" or "improved." Have you ever driven past a business that proudly propertied, "Under new management"? These are reengagement attempts on behalf of a product or service with the goal of communicating with its current customers; *we are improving while attempting to capture new customers.* The idea behind the concept is that people want the latest and greatest. A company can make their product stand out by marking it new or improved.

Schein (2011) states, "Whether or not a culture is 'good' or 'bad,' 'functionally effective,' or not, depends not on the culture alone, but on the relationship of the culture to the environment in which it exists" (Kindle location, 745). Therefore, there is a time to create a fresh look to grab the attention of those who are not engaged and inspire those within the church who are sold out to the ministry. Finding the right place to create a fresh look, or multiple fresh looks is essential to communicating the message of the overall strategy.

The new look is to communicate that the church is improving, growing, and you need to be part of it. The longer any business or organization has been in operation, the more it begins to blend into the nebulous background of ambiguity and obscureity, especially if it is not fighting for relevancy in the community. Our minds have the most advanced process of prioritizing the greatest pertinent information to us, assimilating all the information we sense, see, and hear, either into the consciously engaged category or subconsciously overlooked category.

When something looks the same way it has for years, there is no natural motivation to take a new look at it. Our minds already know that item or entity and its role of relevance, in our lives. If we have forgotten about it, then the thing in question is neither urgent nor relevant from our peripheral prioritization perspective. The fact is when there is no external or internal change people become blind to the church's relevancy in their lives, and it fades into the background of the noise all around them. To the disengaged, it is just another building they pass in route to their busy lives. Therefore, the church must be intentional about delivering an innovative and creative change.

Whether online or onsite, your fresh look will reprioritize your church from the viewpoint of the newcomer and provide those within the church a better way to reference your ministry and the internal growth that is taking place. A new look simultaneously helps with external adaptation and internal integration of the overall strategy for growth.

The framework of redoing any look deals with the concept of innovation and creativity and how these words strengthen the church, its message, and its mission. Oster (2011) defines innovation as, "The intentional development of a specific product, service, idea, environment, or process for the generation of value" (Kindle location, 125). Part of the goal of this phase of the "Refocus" process is to generate value. The church has value; it is the only entity for which Christ Jesus died. This value generation is not the value of the church to

God, but rather the value of the church to those far from God, as well as those who attend the church regularly.

Among the operative words in Oster's salient definition is "intentional development."

Look at everything about your church through the eyes of the disengaged.

As you look at everything that an outsider would see from the curb appeal of your building to the level of clutter in your nursery, to the appearance on your stage, ask the question what message is unintentionally being sent with the aesthetics of these different environments?

Everything about your facility, website, and social media presence, or lack thereof sends a message. If the clear message from all these platforms is the message that needs to be sent to reach your stated objectives and grow, then that is a win. If, however, there are unintentional messages that are being sent by your classrooms and restrooms, social media, and street appeal, then the intentional development of these environments through the lens of creativity and innovation is a must.

Make no mistake; you are sending a message. Much of the time, we become blind to details when we see the same sight on a regular basis. Have you ever been to someone's office, where you literally can't see the desk because of the stuff piled up? If you are like me, you are thinking, *how can a person work in that environment?* The reality is that it does not bother the person with the messy desk because they no longer see it as messy. They are blind to the disordered desk.

When it comes to the church, its facilities, and its website, we too can become blind to the chipping paint and the overgrown shrubs, as well as the archaic web presentation. We can become blind to the cluttered stage and outdated looks. That is why it is essential to walk through your online and onsite environments asking the question, what message does this communicate to someone new?

Innovation and creativity are essential to communicate the message of value and relevance to your community. Michalko (2001) noted, "Creativity is not an accident, not something that is genetically determined. It is not the results of something easily learned, but the consequence of your intention to be creative and your determination to learn and use creative-thinking strategies."

Oster and Michalko highlight the central aspect of an innovative, entrepreneurial mindset. This mentality is something that should be engaged as a church seeks to rebuild post COVID. The efficacious leader intentionally and system-atically creates and innovates. Innovation must be valued enough to make the process of innovation a system, and a discipline. Creativity is not the result of arbitrary general activity, but rather the residual of specific, disciplined nuances of approach to the desired future.

At the church where I lead, creativity is one of our core values and as such during the weekly staff meeting, we go twice around the table. The first time is to cover general staff detail. The second round is just called creative. This is a discipline, that forces us to look through the eyes of our creative God at everything we are doing and ask, *how could it be done?*

Some may push back and say, "I am just not creative." However, sheer determination to innovate, and celebrate inno-vation within the organization creates the opportunity for a culture of innovation. Creative is not something you are it is something you continually do. Saying you are not creative is tantamount to saying you are not spiritual. While witnessing to people, I have been given the excuse many times, "Well I am just not a spiritual person." This line has obviously worked on other people in the past to shut down, a person from sharing their faith. However, as people who study the word of God, we know nothing could be further from the truth. We are more spiritual than we are physical, as this physical; the body will die one day, and our spiritual being will live eternally. I have heard it said, we are not physical beings having a temporary spiritual experience, but rather spiritual beings having a temporary physical experience."

What they are saying is "I do not do spiritual things," but that does not make them any less of a spiritual being. So, to those who would say, "I am just not creative," what they are really saying is "I don't do creative things." The fact is you are creative. You are made in the image of the most creative entity in the universe. (*Genesis 1:26, NLT*). You have the mind of Christ in you. (*1 Corinthians 2:16, NLT*).

Change the way you think, drawing from the Holy Spirit's power, and begin to mirror the majesty of your Maker. Empowered by His Spirit, guided by His Word, and emboldened by the mission, we should be like the sons of Issachar. I Chronicle 12:32 states, "There were 200 leaders from the tribe of Issachar. All of these men understood the signs of their times and new the best course for Israel to take." (*NLT*).

We do not lead in a vacuum we lead in our context. You are empowered by the Holy Spirit to lead just as the sons of Issachar, understanding your time. That means that you are creative, you just must create. Davila, Epstein, and Shelton (2006) state, "One of the first rules of innovation is that you must clearly decide how your organization is going to play the innovation game" (Kindle location, 1634). It is incumbent upon the organizational structure to set the rules for the change game to be rewarding of the innovative aspirant.

On Purpose

Innovation and creativity are not an end, but rather an effective and efficient way to achieve an end. Without a clear goal, attempting to be innovative and creative is idle energy. Creativity and innovation become strategic when they are aligned to accomplish a goal. Innovation by its very nature must have a practical usage or application. Without individuals and organizations having clearly understood and repeatable objectives an innovation is not sustainable. Innovation never takes place in vacuity; it always must be part of a solution, which drives growth and communicates effective change.

Collins and Porrasa (2002) indicate, "One of the most important steps you can take in building a visionary company is not an action, but a shift in perspective" (Kindle location, 1041). This perspective shift toward innovation will not be effective without a clear grasp of the organizational objectives; one's perspective can shift beyond the scale and scope of the organizational values. Therefore, innovation must be anchored in organizational goals.

Michalko (2006) states, "Before you start looking for ideas you need to know your goal" (Kindle location, 547).

A vanguard of individual innovation is one who personally challenges the stagnant growth or declining disciplines in his or her life. The same universal characteristic applies when he or she is leading an innovative initiative across an organizational structure. Collins (2001) indicated, "Greatness is not a function of circumstance. Greatness, it turns out, is largely a matter of conscious choice" (Kindle location, 214). There is a conscientious choice within an individual, and certainly within a group, to resist the tide of innovative apathy or organizational atrophy.

Kouzes and Posner (2012) state, "Leaders, venture out; they don't sit idly by waiting for fate to smile on them" (p. 12). Leading others to venture out is a central requirement to challenging the status quo. The failure to do so is organizational sabotage. Collins and Porras (2002) note, "The only truly reliable source of stability is a strong inner core, and the willingness to change and adapt everything except that core" (Kindle location, 201). The effectual leader must lead the outlook of challenging the ordinary to innovate the extraordinary. The greatest innovations have come to those who perpetually challenge the normative thoughts and comfortable patterns of structure within their organization.

The only element that is allowed to remain unchanged is our values; everything else must be challenged. Collins and Porras

(2002) state, "Indeed if there is one secret to an enduring great company, it is the ability to manage continuity and change-a discipline that must be consciously practiced, even by the most visionary of companies." (Kindle location, 102). The continuity Collins and Porras speak of are a static vision of your core values, the "why" behind the "what," and the "how" of your church.

The innovative process is driven by questions. A relentless question asker is one who has a constant flow of fresh information. The more information an individual or organization has, the greater the solution pool becomes. Oster (2011) notes, "The only way to get better ideas is to get more ideas, and an organization's ability to acquire new ideas and innovate is constrained by the limits of rational boundaries" (Kindle location, 1275).

Oster is suggesting a vast funnel of ideas. As the information makes its way down the funnel, irrelevant concepts will often be eliminated by the core values. However, many in organizational leadership turn the funnel upside-down, with a narrow entry point of ideas and information.

The Oster Funnel

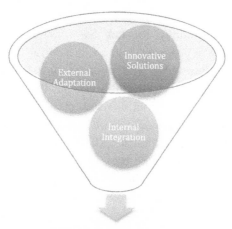

Strategic Innovation

The typical ideation process is inverted, with fewer questions asked perpetually. Often, leaders who have an inverted innovation funnel have a narrow intake of information. Either by philosophy or by hierarchy, churches can use the inverted innovation funnel, erroneously thinking that only the one or few at the head of the church have the best ideas and information regarding the church. This narrow scope limits innovation by inverting Oster's Funnel. Therefore, the volume of information and ideas do not create the opportunity to position the church to reach more people and build organizational commitment, but instead, starts with limited information and leads to diluted ideas.

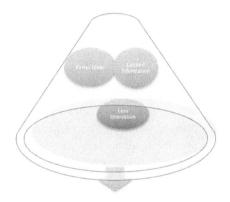

Status Quo

Strategic innovation takes place when the volume of information and ideas are allowed to filter through the core values, align with the objectives, and stimulate ideation for strategy. When a leader models a wide funnel of information at the top, this will be disseminated throughout the organization, and the employees will become perpetual information gatherers.

Don't Fail to Fail

An innovative leader is willing to fail, and an innovative organization must develop a culture of being willing to fail. Once a church reaches a certain age or size, there is a decrease in some of the higher-risk ventures, which ultimately put them in a place of prominence from the start. The attitude of being willing to fail and allowing ideas and people to fail is essential to organizational innovation.

Many times, both individuals and churches fear failure, so they fail to act. Ackermann and Eden (2011) refer to this fear as "paralysis by analysis" (Kindle location, p. 8). Paralysis by analysis takes place when the fear of failure is greater than the fear of dying. Paralysis by analysis takes yesterday's solutions and uses them to confront tomorrow's challenges. Paralysis by analysis is a cyclical process and at its core is the fear of failure. This cycle has a blinding effect on it.

The church can get so caught up in the cycle that it forgets about its mission and buries the head of the organization in the proverbial sand. Stetzer and Dodson (2007) site, the number one problem of church growth, is "Most churches love their traditions more than they love the lost" (p. 61). The impetus for paralysis by analysis is often the church holding on to something of emotional value in the preference spectrum, and not being willing to let go of preference, even it is its trumped by a principle.

Part of the way a leader can pull a church out of a paralysis by analysis cycle is to begin to teach the team to decide when to decide. For example, let's say the church leadership has agreed to redo its exterior and three options that have been vetted by the necessary groups. Essential participants in a venture such as this should always include professional opinions.

If there is a professional in the particular field the decision is revolving around, always begin with their opinion. Don't redo a website without first talking to leading professionals; don't redo landscaping without first consulting a professional land-scape designer. When in a cycle of indecision, lead people to decide when to decide. Simply stated, "We have enough facts, we are going to decide on this date, regarding this matter," This the path to break the cycle of indecision. Berkun (2010), states

"Any seemingly grand idea can be divided into an infinite series of smaller, previously known ideas" (Kindle location 172).

Davila, Epstein, & Shelton (2013) state, "Innovation systems are established policies, procedures, and information mechanisms that facilitate the innovation process within and across organizations" (Kindle location, 2551). One way a church can establish innovation systems is by structuring innovation on the calendar. Snyder and Duarte (2008) state, "Embedding innovation in processes and procedures creating the innovation machine- is only half of the battle. Innovations are truly embedded only when it lives in the hearts and minds of people" (Kindle location, 155).

Imagine the ideas that you could generate if you set aside four days a year, one day per quarter with only one goal, innovation. I recommend going somewhere offsite; a different place and pace can ignite a different perspective. Start the day off with prayer. Review your "why" and "what," your values, and your objectives, but instead of going into your strategies, try brainstorming.

Brainstorming is where the Oster Funnel takes on a powerful function. The rules during these times are simple, no shooting inside the tent. Let every idea fly; there will be a time for practical assimilation. However, the first stage is all about volume. Shooting inside the tent of ideation means pistol-packing naysayers shoot down ideas for their reasons or by their negative analysis. Some ideas during these seasons will be out of range and will not stick. However, those that do will have the ability to empower the church to best leverage its resources to seize on the opportunities and thwart the threats of tomorrow.

By making these days a regular part of your praxis, you can begin to systemize innovation and integrate it into your culture. As the leader, you should know what your chief challenges and threats are going into these days, and then augment your strategies and the ideation that arises from the Oster Funnel.

Michalko (2011) states, "By changing your perspective, you expand your possibilities until you see something that you were unable to see before" (Kindle location 169). With a new angle on ideation, innovation, and creativity, go back to the questions regarding what messages your onsite and online looks are sending. I can suggest a range of areas you can pour creativity and innovation through, however, your contextualization of these ideas is more important than the ideas I will recommend.

Kid's Space

One of the main reasons why new families choose a church is because of what the new church has to offer their kids. Before the music begins, before the sermon has begun, the prospect has concluded their willingness to come back based on the environment and interactions within the first five minutes. The majority of this decision calculous is decided for and by the kids themselves. Williams (1999) calls the notion of kids deciding the direction, "The inside champion" (p. 22).

Williams illustrates the inside champion by taking you inside of a minivan, as a family is deciding which drive-through restaurant to use for take-out. The inside champion is created by the restaurant that has the most favorable prize tucked away inside of a kid's meal. For the kids in the car to drive the decision, they have to be informed and influenced by the restaurant regarding what toy they are offering. In other words, the restaurant does not have to influence the parents, it reaches the kids, and the kids drive the choice.

In many ways, kids can be the inside champion for the church as well. Therefore, creating a new look for your kid's space is time and money that will pay dividends in your retention of the people who visit your church. This new look can start with the entrance to the kid's space or the main stage of the kid's space. When you utilize the Oster Funnel, you can conceive many great and inexpensive ways to create a fresh look on these spaces, which have a high return on retention because if done well, they will build inside champions.

When you are exploring new looks, consider outside environments that do a great job of making that demographic excited to be there such as theme parks, shopping experiences, and other churches' environments that have great spaces. "Create a look" may be a new concept for some on your team, so it is helpful to look at kids' church environments online at what other churches have done and when possible, visit a church that has done a stellar job of leveraging creativity and innovation into different spaces.

Giving your kids space a fresh look is well worth the planning and the funneling or raising of resources needed to do it right. There are several companies that focus on kid's space design and build, that are well worth your time. Innovation is all they do, and they focus that energy on creating an environment that is a magnet for families. At the church I lead we just completed a kid's space redesign; you can explore what that might look like here. https://citychurch.live/children

As you begin to search, you may get overwhelmed, as there are some extensive and expensive setups. You are looking to stimulate ideas, not emulate them. After some searching, begin to ask questions about what resources you have at your disposal. As well as asking the question what resources can I raise? It is better to take on entrance and make it a win than to do a total environment in a mediocre way.

Online Space

Most people visit online before they visit in person. COVID dramatically molded this trend into the hard reality for today. People want to know what they are getting themselves into before they come. They will want to listen to the music, maybe even a few minutes of a sermon. From these few elements, people make a judgment to see if the church is worth a visit. Because of this, one prominent place to give a fresh look is on your website. Davila, Epstein, and Shelton (2013) state, "Successful organizations combine technological change and business model change to create innovation" (Kindle location,

121). Technology has become such an inseparable part of our culture, and as such, this is not a field that can be ignored.

While most churches do not have the luxury of a video department, it is well worth the investment to pay someone to film one of your big weekends and use the footage to make a compelling video of what your ministry has to offer. Some people have not and may not come back from COVID. Churches must begin to plan and prepare to get all their messages online. If video quality is a problem, and it usually is. Start by making audio sermons available consistently and professionally.

Do not put music on the audio or video unless you have set up a DAW, or Digital Audio Workstation.

Music must be mixed separately than the house for it to sound excellent. Churches without a D.A.W. may have great quality worship in the live service, but if it is not mixed for online listening separately, then it will be a detractor instead of an attracter.

The church website should renew its look at least every other year, and every year when resources are available. Technology is advancing so quickly, and this is the only way to stay the most accessible to those looking for a church. Canton (2015) states, "We are living in an era best characterized by radical, complex, and accelerated change. It is the central driver of the future" (p.3).

There are many ways to keep a fresh look digitally that costs little to nothing. One way is to place someone in charge of your social media. Make it their ministry, invest in them, and develop an overarching strategy for leveraging this industry-changing medium. Have them post a couple of scriptures per week related to the Sunday morning message. Use pictures and video whenever possible of outreaches and activities. At the end of the post ask an open-ended question to inspire engagement. Make sure the person you have in place to head this effort is committed to responding to that engagement.

Catmull (2014) states, "Find, develop, and support good people, and they, in turn, will find, develop, and own good ideas" (Kindle location, 1243). While developing a website is a professional skill set, managing social media can be done by anyone that is trusted, and knows the heart of the house and is willing to build community. Ackermann and Eden (2004) state, "Effective organizational change relies upon incrementalism, upon many small wins, rather than the single big win" (p. 9). Through creativity and innovation, the church can systematically create small successes that will build momentum making it easier to accomplish its stated objectives.

Conclusion

Creating a new look is about messaging and momentum. This phase is exciting because much of the stages of "Refocus" are internal adjustments. However, this phase is a change you can see. Creating a new look will give those who have previously committed to the organization a new reference point as they invite people. They will be excited to add to their normal invitation, "We just got through renovating our kids' space, your kids will love it."

Typically, it is not one message that makes the difference, but multiple messages that add up to direct influence. For the person who has driven by your facility for the last decade without a second thought of its relevance to his or her life, when they see a new look on the outside coupled with a personal invite of someone they know, it is at that point where influence begins to grow. The disengaged person begins to think; *maybe I do need to check out this place.*

Most salient to these conversations is the role that creativity and innovation take on as you begin to look at your spaces with fresh eyes. You need to understand it is godly to be creative and to innovate. God is the most creative entity in the universe. When you and I begin to draw upon that creativity and innovation to advance His church, then His blessing over the attributes of innovation and creativity are exponentially leveraged to affect change that alters people's eternity.

Kids' spaces and online spaces are just a couple of examples of new looks you can create. Through leveraging innovation and creativity, you can begin to build momentum in the areas of highest return. A fresh look empowers those with organizational commitment and gets the attention of those who do not yet have a relationship with God or the church.

Why should the best ideas of innovation come from Silicon Valley? Why should the most creative messaging come from a mouse wearing gloves? God has given His only Son to save His lost sons and daughters. We have the genius of God living inside of us every waking moment. Once we are given the commission to create by the Creator, there is no limit to the level of innovation we can step into as the church. The best ideas always belong to God. I believe He is desperately trying to give them to you. What if the turnaround of your church was waiting for you as leaders to be willing to trust God to do something new for you?

What is normal in this generation was once considered impossible in the previous. With great regularity and little international attention, we humans regularly send people into space. We type a message into a box on our computer, and it is instantly transmitted around the globe to terminate in a specified email inbox. We can broadcast a live video from a handheld device that can be seen all over the world.

If all of that can be generated and developed by people who are not filled with the Spirit of God, imagine what a group of God-honoring, Jesus-focused people can do at your church, if you dare to create and innovate and let God change the culture and the way it sees the church through you. I believe the best ideas have yet to be conceived. I believe the greatest innovations have yet to be envisaged.

Post COVID, God has placed you as a difference maker, and leader. Therefore, He has ordained, equipped, empowered, and enabled you to lead the needed change. Take Oster's Funnel approach to your next leadership meeting and begin to allow the genius of God to materialize in the work of His church. Scripture says, "Now to him who can do immeasurably more than all we ask or imagine, according to His power that is at work within us," (*Ephesians 3:20, NIV*).

Chapter Seven

Undergo Strategic Training

There has been more wholesale change through COVID than any other two-year period in my lifetime. Therefore, strategy has never been more important as you approach leading change. There is a three-legged stool upon which this phase of the Post COVID Church sits. If you remove one of the legs, the phase will not stand up on its own, much less support the training your church needs to undergo. The three-legged stool is becoming a *design thinking, leadership development, and learning church*. Strategic training is the intentional, goal-oriented, growth process that leverages available resources toward articulated objectives. Strategic training starts with the end in mind and builds a development and design thinking system that places the church on a perpetual path of learning what is necessary to fulfill its strategic interest.

Design Thinking

Brown (2009) states, "Design thinking relies on our ability to be intuitive, to recognize a pattern, to construct ideas that have an emotional meaning as well as functionality" (Kindle location, 93). This intuition that is spoken of in the business world would be better translated for the church and the direction of the Holy Spirit. Along with His other divine duties, the Holy Spirit is our "Paraclete." John, quoting Jesus, wrote, "And I will ask the Father, and he will give you another Advocate, who will never leave you. He is the Holy Spirit, who leads into all truth. The world cannot receive him because it isn't looking for him and doesn't recognize Him. But you know Him because He lives with you now and later will be in you" (*John 14:16-17, NLT*).

The Greek word for Comforter is *parakletos*, from the verb *parakaleo*. The word for *"Paraclete"* is passive in form, and etymologically signifies "called to one's side" (Orr, 1913). Therefore, the Holy Spirit will be your best coach and counselor as you begin the design thinking process. He will give you intuition to "lead you into all truth."

We can do a lot after we pray, but we can do very little until we pray. Start off this process by tapping into the best executive and ecclesial coach there has ever been, the Holy Spirit. Will you dare to ask Him to open your eyes to what needs to change within your church so that you can be the best representation of Christ in the world that you can be? Are you bold enough to be willing to sacrifice some of your personal preferences on the altar of your mission? If so, then let the Holy Spirit come alongside you in this design thinking phase.

Cunningham (2015) argues, "The first principle of corporate culture is the tone at the top" (p. 1). When the level of thinking and learning at the top disseminates through the cultural undercurrent of the organizational structure, it affects the operational sector of the ministry as long as the way of thinking is communicated consistently. This communication is both formal and informal.

Formal communication is in the form of mottos, slogans, mission statements, and sermon series that support the intuition of design thinking. Informal communication is related to the back channels of influence where people within the church model the methodology of those at the top. Therefore, if design thinking is modeled and formally communicated, then it will be emulated throughout the organizational structure.

Informal communication of design thinking is not just the leader learning, but it is also the intentionality by which that leader indoctrinates learning into the organizational structure. If, however, a leader is not taking the initiative to develop that culture, then he or she will have the culture dedicated to the lowest common denominator.

Design thinking starts with the values, funneling through the objectives, and reviewing the strategies to determine what learning, training, or development needs to be for the stated goals to be met. The communication element of design thinking is the key to drive those learning objectives all the way down to the operational levels of the church. Gabler (2006) noted, "Part of Walt Disney's secret was that he insisted on quality from individuals of whom it had never been required, he inspired commitment" (Kindle location, 2902). Disney wanted his design thinking to touch every single element of the customers' experience. He did not limit his thinking to well-planned parks, but wanted all of his staff, from the executive to the street sweeper, to emanate design thinking of creating "magic." For this "magic" to be sustained, the communication of that design thinking had to be seamlessly embraced through all of the cogs of operations.

Magic for Disney is a word that works the design down into the functional fabric of the organization. They teach their employees at all levels that their goal is to create magic for every guest experience. This communication works because every person can envision how they can elevate the guest experience of everyone they encounter.

One day we went to Disney to celebrate my Dad's and our middle son, Cruz's, birthday. As you may know, when you attend a Disney Park on your birthday, they give you a birthday pin. All day long throughout the park, shouts came both from Disney Park employees and guests alike, "Happy Birthday, Cruz! Happy Birthday, Jim!"

That alone makes you want to go back and spend every birthday with Mickey. One simple system of identifying guests with a special occasion, and training the employees to shout, "Happy Birthday!" with the person's name is the perfect example of design thinking that accomplishes Disney's goal of creating magic.

Disney's example of design thinking which can be seen in a

barrage of other elements, also illustrates the emotional part of the communication. The employees yelled my son's and Dad's names so frequently that other guests began to chime in as well. The customer contributed to the magic. Liedtke & Ogilvie, (2011) stated, "Great designers inspire - they grab us on an emotional level" (Kindle location, 184). This type of design thinking embodies what the church should seek to accomplish through design thinking.

Liedtke & Ogilvie (2011) state, "Growth is ultimately about solving the customers' problems. Even if they do not have one yet" (Kindle location, 499). For The Post COVID Church, growth is ultimately about solving the church's missiology problems, even if it does not have them yet. All churches post COVID have a common problem. Many people who were coming before, have quit coming.

When it comes to design thinking, we must learn to break things before they are broken. If we wait until things are broken, then it will cost more time and resources to fix the problem then.

Internal growth, by its very nature, stretches the capacity of the leaders, systems, as it intentionally and intuitively develops training that ultimately brings external growth. This design thinking system feeds the desired internal culture and starves the behavior disruptive to organizational growth. Schein (2010) states, "The culture of a group can now be defined as a pattern of shared basic assumptions learned by a group as it solved its problems of external adaptation and internal integration, which has worked well enough to be considered valid and, therefore, to be taught to new members as the correct way to perceive, think, and feel in relation to those problems" (Kindle location, 447).

This pattern of shared basic assumptions can be intentional, thus fulfilling the stated organizational objectives. Conversely, the pattern can be unintentional and as such be driven by political, preferential, or circumstantial elements. It is the organizational equivalent of being on a boat in the middle of an ocean without a way to navigate the vessel. The ship would be a victim of the winds and waves, as opposed to harnessing those elements to steer the boat in the desired direction. Design thinking charts a course and teaches a way of thinking that harnesses the internal and external elements to end up at the desired location.

Organizations that intentionally grow, strategically train. Michelli (2007) states "In stunning contrast to most Fortune 500 companies, Starbucks consistently spends more on training than it does on advertising" (p.11). For churches, this training must be modeled by those at the top, and mirrored by all of those on the operational level, albeit the nursery worker, the parking lot attender, and or the greeters.

Brown (2009) notes, "Design thinking is fundamentally an exploratory process; done right, it will invariably make unexpected discoveries along the way" (p. 16). What unexpected discoveries is your church waiting to make? Buried below the mundane and lurking just beneath the surface of the recurring problems are unexpected discoveries that will bring refreshment to your church and refinement to your vision. When you see a problem for the second time, it is the emergence of a pattern. Behind every problematic pattern is a pragmatic solution. Once defined as a recurring problem, design thinking goes to work to improve your church systematically.

Canton (2015) indicates, "Trends are the hidden forces that shape the future. Trends are the reflection of how change manifests and transforms our lives, work, entertainment, competition, and health" (p. 5). When the design thinker knows what he or she is looking for, the force is more apparent than not. The force is only hidden from the uninformed or those who do not want to change. Once a church leader has been made aware of the forces of change, trend identification becomes second nature.

Canton (2015) further states, "Trends are born of forces

converging to create a new market, product, lifestyle, or culture. Trends shape new expressions of reality that provide risks and opportunity" (p. 5). Identifying the sources behind the behavioral or cultural patterns of your church will inform your design thinking. Schein (2010) states, "Culture as a set of basic assumptions defines for us what to pay attention to, what things mean, how to react emotionally to what is going on and what actions to take in various kinds of situations" (p. 29). How behavior affects internal trends is cultural, in nature and how design thinking affects behavior provides the leader with the solutions to use the winds and waves of culture to navigate the vessel to the desired destination. Phillips (2012) indicates, "The first step in defining an innovative process is spotting trends" (p. 59).

The design thinker not only has his or her finger on the pulse of the church, but additionally, their eyes on the horizon of their external environment. Kurmar (2013) calls this "Sense Intent" saying "The sense intent mindset is about continuously detecting the latest changes happening in the world today and formulating new speculations about what new situations may be looming on the horizon" (Kindle location, 602). This mode is essential to innovative development because it is the open front door through which trends and super trends intersect with a creative process. A trend is a pattern of change; a super trend is the convergence of two or more patterns of change that creates a new force of transformation that is greater than the individual trends operating in isolation.

If your church were a house, there are windows and a backdoor through which information can flow. However, what is out in front, and emerging will come through the front door first, and then cascade throughout the rest of the innovative structure. Kumar, (2013) notes "The goal of this mode is to provide sufficient early direction for research and exploration" (Kindle location, 602).

Kumar (2013) states, the innovative organization must view "...Sensing changing conditions, as a mindset" (Kindle location, 614). One could consider the volume of information that is filtered and prioritized by the human brain. Lewis (2015) notes, "The Thalamus is thought to be a kind of relay where sensory neurons meet and are sent to their destination in the cerebral cortex." The Thalamus is the "Sense Intent" of the human brain. Lewis (2015) indicates, "When the cortex receives a type of information that it deems a priority (like focusing on the movie), it sends a signal back to a part of the thalamus known as the reticular nucleus." The body is not only constantly receiving information, but it is also filtering it and prioritizing it.

Likewise, churches must be on the constant lookout for opportunities and threats within the emerging change in their communities. The filters are set by the stated objectives of the church, and the systems can be built to prioritize the emerging change or to deprioritize the information coming in. Ursrey (2014) argues, "Design thinking combines creative and critical thinking that allows information and ideas to be organized, decisions to be made, situations to be improved, and knowledge to be gained. It's a mindset focused on solutions."

Design thinking is at its best when it is solving problems, and as such, this question should be asked.

Can our current church model solve our current church problems?

If not, then design thinking is the only perceivable way out of a present predicament. Brown (2009) indicates, "The continuum of innovation is best thought of as a system of three overlapping spaces. Inspiration, the problem or opportunity that motivates the search for solutions; ideation, the process of generating, developing, and testing ideas; and implementation" (p. 16).

For churches, the final stage is the most frequent "overlapping space" to be left undone as it deals with change, not in a theoretical manner, but a practical one. Testing ideas and implementing them is difficult for churches that have become behaviorally stuck. It is in the phases where the desire to live out the mission of the church must exceed the pain of change within the church. Hamel (2002) states, "Delay is deadly" (p. 56). This sentiment is most certainly applicable to this overlapping space.

Leadership Development

Leadership development is the deliberate and ongoing quantifiable path in which an organization builds its future through growing its leaders. When leadership development is absent, there is the presence of leader slip. Leaders begin to slip into the vacuum of their macro agendas and micro passions, which never holistically drive the organization forward. Compression is the key to compulsion. In an engine, the combustion chamber is made up of the cylinder, piston, and cylinder head. An engine generates power from the expansion of compressed air. If this air were not compressed, it would not have the power to drive the engine. Therefore, compression is the key to compulsion.

The same is true with a holistic planning and execution of leadership development. If the development is not focused on the organizational objectives, then it will lose compression, resulting in discouraged leaders and unmet expectations. Hughes, Beatty, and Dinwoodie (2014) state, "In practical terms the organizational strategy, the vision, the directions, and the tactics adopted to move toward success ought to be held in an ongoing state of formulation, implementation, reassessment, and revision." (p. 4) Compressing the development of leadership into the targeted area of needed growth conversely generates the power to drive the engines of momentum and growth.

There is a difference between leader development and leadership development. Leader development is the systematic growth and optimization of an individual's potential through goal-centric modules that yield a measurable outcome. Leadership development is the systematic growth of the accumulative capacity of the team through goal-centric modules that yield measurable outcomes. Van Velsor, McCauley, and Ruderman (2010) state, "The development of strategic leadership must happen not just at the individual level, but at the team and organizational levels as well" (Kindle location, 344). Vital to your church's revitalization is the growth of her leader and leadership. Stetzer and Dodson (2007) state, "Leadership was rated as the number one factor by the churches that experienced revitalization" (P.34).

Van Velsor, McCauley, and Ruderman, (2010) state, "Developmental methods can be organized into five categories, *developmental relationships, developmental assignments, feedback process, formal programs, and self-development activities*" (p. 44). Drawing from this framework is a good starting point for the module construct of the developmental processes. You should create modular learning within each part of this framework to incrementally reshape the functional mode necessary to ignite internal and external growth.

Developmental Relationships

Ask yourself, *what are some ways that we can develop the necessary relationships that will drive internal growth?* There may be factions in the church with both "sides" entrenched in their preferential concepts. When there is little growth happening, these "sides" take on a life of their own. The two conflicting perspectives can be contemporary versus traditional, Sunday school versus small groups, youth group versus senior's citizen groups.

For the church to move forward, these influence blocks must become a cohesive cog that drives the engine of revitalization forward.

If there are opposing groups, then schedule some relational time dedicated to refocusing the group on its shared objectives. Internal relationship development is vital to unearthing the treasure of shared priority and focusing on that, as opposed to the marginal differences.

Additionally, external relationships are also critical to develop. These relationships may be with community leaders, but most importantly, church leaders that are cultivating their churches to grow. I went on a weight loss journey. I lost over 60 pounds in several years. One of the things I did in the midst of that journey is I began to hang out with people who lived healthily. I stopped going to buffets and started going to the gym. I knew if I only spent time with people who viewed food the way I had seen food, it would be more difficult to change.

The same is true in the church revitalization world. There are those who will help you create excuses for why things are the way they are and will never change. Then there are those with a different mindset. Some relationships will challenge you, and there are relationships that will enable you. The leadership of the church must turn off the enabling and comfortable relationships and seek out those who are growing. Find new relationships, and you will find new life.

I recommend an onsite visit to a church on a growth path that you admire. Bring as many of your team members as you can afford and connect them with the growing church's counterparts. Fostering these types of relationships are far more valuable than attending yet another conference. An onsite visit is a relational development tool that can spur ongoing growth through dynamic relationships in a context that is inspirational in its setting.

Developmental Assignments

After an in-depth look at the basic assumptions of the church, its behavioral patterns, and internal culture, areas of needed growth will emerge. We will call them cultural constraints. These areas may have been identified in the evaluation phase. However, the developmental assignment is where you prioritize internal growth that will affect external growth. Take no less than five areas of growth and plan two-month modules wherein you strategically lead the team through personal and group growth assignments in the area of needed change. The assignments need to be a variety of measurable requirements that approach development from an asymmetrical platform. These assignments will include books for the team to read followed by blog posts they will write on the topic. When you move the team from the learning to teaching phase, there is much more internalization and contextualization of the needed information.

Additionally, teaming groups together to make a short presentation of their shared findings will build comradery as well as take internal growth to the next level.

Another element may include planning a leadership event for the lay leadership with the themes that are being explored. Any additional layering you can do with the needed change slowly erodes the entrenched behaviors and philosophies that inhibit growth and establishes momentum for the desired change.

Feedback Processes

Recently, while traveling through the Atlanta airport, I saw something interesting while exiting the restroom. It was a small, computerized station that had a question on its display, "How did we do?" Below this caption was a smiley face, an ambivalent face, and a sad face. I remember thinking we need these as people exit the church. While admittedly there are some days that I wouldn't want to know the results, the question is interesting. Feedback is your friend, not your foe. Our approach to feedback will determine the speed with which we adapt to the needed principles and practices that will create lasting growth. You as leaders set the tone and tenor of feedback. Start by eliciting feedback from your congregants. Find a strong constructive element and intentionally apply the feedback toward needed change and make certain everyone knows it was a suggestion.

Affirming the process of feedback and the value of feedback is vital to internal growth. Michelli (2007) quotes Starbuck's Howard Schultz, "Customers feel betrayed when they are lured into believing that their input matters, only to find out that their preferences are ignored" (P. 29). Feedback from your parishioners must be taken seriously, and you must look for the opportunity to affirm the severity of their opinion.

Secondly, feedback systems should be implemented for the team from the leader. People want to know what the expectations are and if they are in fact being met. Feedback from the top leadership to the functional fabric is essential to motivate the behavior that is desired to spur growth. People will do what you perpetually celebrate. For this reason, positive affirmation in a competitive environment is far more important than critical feedback. There is certainly a time for constructive criticism, however publicly applauding the desired behavior goes way further than publicly criticizing the unwanted behavior.

Blanchard and Hodges (2005) state, "Our leadership legacy is not just limited to what we accomplish, but it includes what we leave behind in the hearts and minds of those with whom we had a chance to teach and work" (Kindle location, 616). By developing the leaders, you are not just growing the church internally, but you are improving and empowering the hearts and minds of those with whom God has called you to work. Challenging is not something you do to your team it is something you do for your team. Blanchard and Hodges (2005) state, "Leading like Jesus is a transformational cycle that begins with personal leadership and then moves to leading others in one-on-one relationships, then leading a team or group, and finally leading an organization or community" (Kindle location, 339).

Formal Programs

Rima (2000) states "Effective organizational leaders can transform existing paradigms and practices through their use of influence and the mobilization of necessary resources to realize something more beneficial and more effective" (Kindle location, 378). Formal programs communicate a core principle through an all-out operation for change. This united front has measurable outcomes that are communicated regularly and emotionally connect with the leadership constituents. Formal programs may be celebrations, posters, t-shirts, or a range of communication pieces that seek to solidify the importance of the initiative further.

Formal programs may be imported from an existing tool or resource. Many programs have a curriculum as well as other resources to execute the development of that idea or behavior. Examples of formal programs are read *The 21 Irrefutable Laws of Leadership,*

Five Dysfunctions of a Team and *Death by Meeting.* Additionally, the greatest example of a formal program is simply taking your team through *Strategic Health* and customizing its applications turning the chapters into modules so you can, in turn, create landmarks as you trek through the Refocus process. Formal programs are important because they present a decided and united front, and as a result that will allow less compression loss in the pistons of the engine of change. The change is focused, celebrated, and mutually beneficial to the leader and the leadership.

Self-development Activities

Scripture says we are to train up a child in the way he or she should go (*Proverbs 22:6, KJV*). The word train in the Hebrew is "Chanak" (Strong's, 2596). "Chanak" is a type of paste that the wet nurses would rub on the top of an infant's mouth to stimulate their hunger to nurse at the desired time of the nurse. In essence, scripture is directing parents to place hunger for the right things, at the right time on the palates of our children. Likewise, as leaders, we are to place the paste of development on the palate of everyone with whom we influence; in doing so, we are developing a hunger for growth and offering our best for the glory of God.

Blanchard and Hodges (2005) further illustrate this parallel by stating, "Most of the leadership that shapes our lives does not come from leaders with titles on an organizational chart; it comes from leaders in our daily life" (Kindle location, 219). Relationships that are built on development last longer and are more effective than a typical top-down relationship. As a leader, if you make your people hungry to develop, you are adding intrinsic value to their life, and they will forever be connected to you.

Self-development activities build strategic thinking. Beatty and Hughes (2005) state, "Strategic thinking includes the cognitive process required for collecting, interpreting, generating, and evaluating information and ideas that shape an organization's enduring success" (p. 61). Development is the combustion that propels an engine, and strategic thinking is the wheels. Once you get the wheels going, it is much easier to steer the church into a faster lane of development.

Self-development activities improve the atmosphere and overall environment of the church. Cameron and Quinn (2006) indicated, "Environment can best be managed through teamwork and employee development" (Kindle location, 748). If you do not manage your environment, your environment will manage you.

Blanchard and Hodges (2005) stated, "Leading like Jesus is a transformational cycle that begins with personal leadership and then moves to lead others in one-on-one relationships, then to lead a team or group and finally, to lead an organization or community" (Kindle location, 339). Everyone within the leadership structure must see leaders at the top modeling all these developmental elements in his or her own life. Kouzes and Posner (2012), expressed "Leading by example are more efficient than leading by command. If people see that you work hard while preaching hard work, they are more likely to follow you." (p. 17). As leaders perpetuate the latent attitudes, motives, and attributes of his or her heart, they will inevitably disseminate those same characteristics throughout the rank and file of their organizational structure. Bekker (n.d.) states, "An organization will only develop what it consistently models."

Van Velsor, McCauley, and Ruderman (2010) argue, "Developing the individual capacities needed for effective leadership such as self-management, social skills, and work facilitation capacities is all synonymous with what is often labeled, 'personal development'" (p. 25). Holistic leadership development will eventually overpower the undercurrent of negative leadership or culture within the group. Momentum overcomes mood, and negativity is replaced with productivity. The church eventually gets to a point in which it changes the preexisting social reliances and alliances as the church gets her sights set on its mission.

As the drivers of the organizational culture shift, the ability for one dominantly negative individual is overridden by the bandwidth of the organizational culture. Van Velsor, McCauley, and Ruderman (2010) state, "Viewing leadership as a collective phenomenon have many implications for leadership development. First, leadership culture rather than the individual leader become the target for leadership development." (Kindle location 1431).

Learning Organization

A learning organization is an entity that views learning as part of its ongoing objectives.

In the graveyard of vision statements and catchy slogans of yesterday lay the organizational cadavers of entities that were once revered as the greats of their day. Their rise to the top was long enough to gain confidences in yesterday's strategies and technologies. However, confidence built by yesterday's success turns into cognitive dissonance; a need for security overrides the drive for innovation; a hunger for knowledge is replaced by a sense of entitlement, and the predictable demise ensues.

This tragedy is the cautionary tale for businesses and organizations, as well as churches who did not remain a learning organization. The reason? Many of the organizations failed to translate the same passion for growing and learning that got them there, into a systematic discipline to perpetuate internal growth.

The final leg of the stool of training is changing the developmental culture so much that it transforms into a learning organization. Churches are not immune to organizational life cycles, trends, or even market dynamics. Therefore, churches must become and remain a learning organization.

Churches that learn are churches that lead. Senge (1994) stated, "To practice, a discipline is to be a lifelong learner on a never-ending development path" (Kindle location, 2184). If there is any organization that should be continually learning it is the church. We have the most important mandate and the most vital mission.

Why do churches stop learning? Gino & Staats (2015) note, "Fear of failure, a fixed mindset, overreliance on past performance, and attribution bias are all reasons why organizations don't learn." The church cannot afford to let any of these reasons hinder its internal growth, especially in light of the present phenomenon of church decline. Bersin (2013) notes, "One of the most important sources of competitive advantage is your entire corporate learning strategy." When the church decides that perpetual internal growth is her business, then perpetual, spiritual, numerical, and financial growth will be its fruit.

Cameron and Quinn (2006) suggest asking questions such as, "What will our organization need to be like to be highly successful in the future? In what areas would we like to be on the leading edge? Where are we currently underdeveloped to reach these objectives? (Kindle location, 1335). Measurable questions about where you need to be will determine how you need to grow.

These types of questions will also help you as a church leader deal with the realities in front of you. Collins (2001) noted, "You must never confuse faith that you will prevail at the end which you can never afford to lose with the discipline to confront the most brutal facts of your current reality, whatever they might be" (Kindle location, 1508). We know the gates of

Hell will not prevail against the church. (*Matthew 16:18, NIV*). Hell will not be victorious over the church in the end, and part of hell not being victorious is God's leaders like you resisting the tide of church decline, making a commitment to grow internally, praying for a fresh vision, and beginning to seek the lost like never before.

Hughes, Beatty, and Dinwoodie (2014) indicate, "The best way for organizations to thrive in the face of new realities is to become a continual learning engine" (p. 3). Becoming a learning organization is signing you and your church up to be continually challenged. Kouzes and Posner (1995) note, "Challenge is the crucible for greatness. Every single personal-best leadership case involved a change from the status quo" (p. 19). While everyone has the opportunity for greatness, not everyone has the will to expand their capacity. The will is informed by core beliefs. In this instance, the core belief says change is fundamental to the survivability and viability of the organization.

Phillips (2012) states, "To remain competitive, firms must increase their innovation capacities instead of playing follow the leader" (p. 8). The same is true of the church world. Who is our competition? The enemy of our souls, this world's system, business, humanism, and the list goes on and on. Learning means understanding our times, understanding our culture, leveraging technology, along with our life-long discipleship journey. Senge (1994) says, "In the long run the only sustainable source of competitive advantage is your organization's ability to learn faster than its competition" (Kindle location, 316).

Knowledge is an attribute that you can obtain only by understanding that you will never fully have it. Knowledge is power, not a possession. One never fully knows because knowledge is growing exponentially. The efficacious leader must never stop growing. Myra and Shelley (2005) note, "Leadership, means plugging away until the breakthrough happens. The energy that it takes to retreat might have been just the amount of energy needed to succeed." (Kindle location, 1701).

In the game of American football, there are two places on each end of the field called the "red zone." These are the last 20 yards a team must carry the ball to score a touchdown. The problem with leadership is there is no defined red zone. There are no markings on the field of ministry to communicate to the leader or the team that you are almost there and need to push harder. So, you as a leader, carrying the ball of the gospel must persist. Keep running, keep praying, keep growing, keep learning, leverage technology, make disciples, and teach them to do the same.

Conclusion

For your church to succeed in training, it must understand and fully implement the three-legged stand of design thinking, leadership development, and being a learning organization. Remove one of these core principles and then the revitalization does not have a stable stool upon which to sit. With these three legs firmly in place, a church in plateau or decline will have the framework to grow from within, which will inevitably lend itself to growing in every way. Internal growth always proceeds external growth.

When the leader at the top models to the team members design thinking, develop and be a preputial learner, then those within the sphere of his or her leadership will do the same. Your church leadership will either define the culture or be confined to an existing culture.

Northouse (2013) states, "Leadership, is a process. Leadership involves influence, leadership occurs in groups, and leadership involves common goals" (Kindle location, 464). Leadership is not a title; it is a responsibility. As you take the responsibly to train your church and your leaders, then you will successfully create growth. Spiritual, financial, and numerical growth happens when there is a hunger for personal growth within the leader.

Learning how to be a design thinker will sharpen your church's focus on discernable patterns and how to leverage available resources to get ahead of opportunities and threats so that you can be best postured for growth. Leadership development is the ongoing process of expanding the potential and capacity of both the individual leader as well as the overall leadership capability. Leadership development sees the strengths of the individual leader and the overall gifts of the church as a platform upon which to build not a stage upon which one has arrived.

Leadership development is all about breaking the cultural goals down into measurable modules, and then creating accountability around progressing through the stated objectives. Becoming a learning organization is really about humility. It is a posture within our hearts that says to God; "Your mission is more important than my comfort." It says we don't know what we don't know and part of our business in making disciples is to be a disciple who grows in every way possible.

Chapter Eight

Serve the Community

In the Leadership world, servant leadership is a phrase that seems counterintuitive. However, a deeper look into the heart behind the heading will open avenues of understanding that emanate from the original servant leader, Jesus. More than any leader in the history of the world, Jesus Christ could have justifiably led through power and domination. His credentials alone placed him in a category that no other could attain; He is the Son of God, the Creator of all of life, He lived a sinless life and built a massive following out of a few teenage fishermen. He displayed power over the demonic and moral high ground over the religious elite.

In three and a half years, he went from total obscurity to the most talked about figure in the history of the world. Jesus is a person about whom more lyrics have been written, more paintings painted, and more speeches delivered than any other. Jesus 'posture toward leadership stood in stark contrast to the leader models of His day. Jesus chose to spend time with sinners over religious leaders, He welcomed children, He empowered women, He sought the broken, the poor, the demon-possessed, and the distressed. Even when those whom He created and He came to die for turned their back on Him, His response was, "Father forgive them for they know not what they do" (*Luke 23:34, NIV*).

The servant heart of Jesus is seen from the moment He opened His eyes on the back side of a Judean barn, to the moment He closed them on the front of a Roman cross. Even after His resurrection, Jesus is seen cooking breakfast for some unsuspecting disciples. Jesus created, modeled, and embodied the servant leader. Jesus did not lead in this manner to be eccentric or to create a niche, but rather this servanthood flowed directly from the heart of God. Jesus was not trying to be a certain way; he was a certain way. Greenleaf (1977) states, "The servant-leader is a servant first. It begins with the natural feeling that one wants to serve, to serve first" (Kindle location, 346).

Jesus' servant leadership is seen clearest on the night before his execution. Mark records,

On the first day of the Festival of Unleavened Bread, when it was customary to sacrifice the Passover lamb, Jesus' disciples asked him, "Where do You want us to go and make preparations for You to eat the Passover?"

So He sent two of his disciples, telling them, "Go into the city, and a man carrying a jar of water will meet you. Follow him. Say to the owner of the house he enters, 'The Teacher asks: Where is My guest room, where I may eat the Passover with My disciples?' He will show you a large room upstairs, furnished and ready. Make preparations for us there." The disciples left, went into the city and found things just as Jesus had told them. So, they prepared the Passover (*Mark 14:12-16 NIV*).

Jesus had arranged for a fully furnished meeting place, then gave the disciples turn by turn directions. All of the details were taken care of by Jesus even down to the schedule of a seemingly random water delivery guy. Jesus told the disciples to make the rest of the preparations there. However, someone dropped the organizational ball. When everyone arrived, there was no servant to clean everyone from their travel. During this time, walking was the predominant means of transportation; in fact, the only time that Jesus was seen not walking was when he rode into Jerusalem on a donkey.

Why a donkey? Why not a white stallion, or a double-humped camel? Jesus riding a donkey was not out of circumstantial convenience, but rather prophetic fulfillment. Zechariah wrote,

Rejoice greatly, Daughter of Zion! Shout, Daughter Jerusalem!
See, your king comes to you, righteous and victorious, lowly and riding on a donkey, on a colt, the foal of a donkey. I will take away the chariots from Ephraim and the warhorses from Jerusalem, and the battle bow will be broken.
He will proclaim peace to the nations. His rule will extend from sea to sea
and from the River to the ends of the earth (*Zechariah 9:9-10, NIV*).

Jesus came riding on a donkey not because it was all they could afford, but because Jesus was making a statement about a kingdom dynamic that shifted the paradigms of human-made leadership. Jesus' statement was clear to those who lined the streets with a shout of "Hosanna, Hosanna, blessed is he who comes in the name of the Lord" (*Luke 19:38, NIV*). In the time and place in which Jesus lived, what a King rode was an indication of his intentions. If he rode a horse, he was coming to make war. Jesus does come riding a horse. However, that is later in the narrative of the man, when he, along with the host of heaven ride to make war against the beast and the kings of the earth (*Revelation 19:19, NIV*). However, Jesus' ride into Jerusalem was to send a different message. When a King rode a donkey, it was for the purpose of proclaiming peace.

While riding a donkey was a prophetic and vivid display of a servant leader, Jesus took the modeling even further with what happened next. The disciples had a furnished room where they made preparations for the feast. However, event planning was not high on these young men's skill set; they forgot a very significant detail, the servant. It was customary to provide someone to wash the feet of those who entered such a celebration. Having someone to wash their feet was just as practical as it was theological.

The Old Testament is replete with precedent for the practice of washing feet before one entered a temple or a dwelling. In the case of the upper room, the need for a foot washing stretched far beyond the practical necessity of cleansing dirty feet from their travel; it took on a spiritual embodiment that cannot be overlooked as the church considers servant leadership.

Have you ever been at work, caught in the midst of that awkward moment when everyone in the organization realized that you dropped the ball? What do you do? Do you call it out, do you pretend as if it does not matter, do you step in and fix it? The problem with stepping in and fixing the situation is it may be beneath your desired station.

You may say to yourself, *if I get the coffee this time then I am forever the coffee guy or gal*. Let someone else do it so that I can maintain my positional clout. That was the sentiment from Jesus' disciples when they realized that no one booked the servant to wash people's feet. Some of the disciples were in the midst of a "who will be second in charge of the Kingdom" dispute, and picking up a servant's towel was the last visual they needed.

However, Jesus stepped forward and broke all of the norms of leadership decorum. Jesus stooped. One of the contestants for second place, John, wrote,

> Jesus knew that the Father had put all things under his power and that he had come from God and was returning to God; so, he got up from the meal, took off his outer clothing, and wrapped a towel around his waist. After that, he poured water into a basin and began to wash his disciples' feet, drying them with the towel that was wrapped around him. (*John 13:3-5, NIV*).

Shocked and stunned was the reaction of all of the disciples. Why was the most powerful man in the universe acting as a bondservant? A bondservant is very different than a slave. Slavery, as practiced in the early years of America's history was ripe with biblical rebuke. Slave trading as referenced in I Timothy 1:9-10 was listed among the most egregious of sins. Slave trading is when someone is free, but they are captured and sold as property. This practice is explicitly condemned by scripture.

However, a bondservant was not a slave, and the most crucial distinction is that a bondservant was not racially selected as opposed to the slave trading in early America that was exclusively rascality oriented. Slave trading stands in stark contrast to a bondservant. Typically, one became a bondservant when they could not pay their debt. Often if the collateral were not available for the one who needed to borrow money, they would sign a statement submitting to being a bondservant for some years if they could not service the debt.

When Peter and John, the two main competitors for the elusive second spot in the Kingdom, were sent to make preparations, both of them failed to book the bondservant, and both of them failed to step up to meet the need. Instead, the leader of the universe took off His seamless garment wrapped a servant's towel around His waist and was doing the job of a bondservant. Jesus was doing the job of someone who owed a debt.

Jesus was making His way around the stunned room when he got to one of the ball droppers. John records, "He came to Simon Peter, who said to him, "Lord, are you going to wash my feet?" Jesus replied, "You do not realize now what I am doing, but later you will understand." "No," said Peter, "you shall never wash my feet" (*John 13: 6-8, NIV*).

Peter was a powerhouse of an individual. He was the first among the disciples to confess Jesus as the Son of God. Peter was the only disciple that walked on water with the Lord. He was at the Mount of Transfiguration and witnessed an ecclesial executive meeting between Jesus, Moses, and Elisha. Yes, Peter would deny the Lord, but after that, he would lead the church's most significant expansion into the Gentile people and beyond (*Acts 10, NIV*).

However, at the last supper, Peter was holding on to his pride, as the hands that formed the stars were reaching to wash his feet. At first, Peter refused to let the Lord wash his feet. John continued, "Jesus answered, "'Unless I wash you, you have no part with me.'" ""Then, Lord," Simon Peter replied, "not just my feet but my hands and my head as well!" (*John 13:9*, NIV). The disciples were still not clear as to what was happening and why. John noted,

> When he had finished washing their feet, he put on his clothes and returned to his place. "Do you understand what I have done for you?" he asked them. "You call me 'Teacher' and 'Lord,' and rightly so, for that is what I am. Now that I, your Lord and Teacher, have washed your feet, you also should wash one another's feet. I have set you an example that you should do as I have done for you. Very truly I tell you, no servant is greater than his master, nor is a messenger greater than the one who sent him. Now that you know these things, you will be blessed if you do them (*John 13:10-17, NIV*).

Rhetorically, Jesus asked the disciples if they understood what he was doing. Next, Jesus referred to his titles, "You call me teacher and Lord." But then Jesus reversed the order of the terms to them calling himself first Lord, then the Teacher. Given that I am your Lord and Teacher I have washed your feet. Next, Jesus provided the reason why he took the place of someone who owed a big debt. Jesus stated, "I have set you an example that you should do as I have done for you." Jesus towel service was the origin of servant leadership, and this is the model the church should emulate as it relates to reaching her communities.

Jesus was not merely modeling a methodology, but a mindset. A servant leader is, first of all, a servant and secondly, a leader. Loving and serving the needs of others is what breaks down the walls built up by a life of sin. Even in the midst of the disciples' ongoing conflict about who was greater, Jesus was breaking down the walls of pride so they could know the heart of the model.

The heart of a servant leader gives unconditional love meeting the needs of those who at the moment, can do nothing for you in return. In this setting, Jesus' disciples proved useless to help him in the hours to come. Although Peter tries to intervene on Jesus' arrest later in the garden by slicing off the ear of the high priest's servant, ultimately, Jesus fate was decided before the foundation of the world. The people Jesus was serving in this upscale Jerusalem venue would not help Jesus at that moment. However, through servant leadership, Jesus tore down the walls in the disciple's lives, and the heart of the leader would infect the hearts of the followers.

The 11 disciples that remained in leadership oversaw the global expansion of the gospel. All over the world, I have met people by the name of Peter, James, and John. Their influence is still shaping society nearly two-thousand-years later. Why? Love broke through in the upper room and established a core value that regardless of the given context, turns the heart of everyone.

When it comes to love, it cannot be systemized. It must be internalized, and as such, it is a seminal function that flows from the heart of the servant leader. The antithesis of love is not to hate, but self-centeredness. One cannot effectively lead an organization that requires people to drive home its values and meets its purposes without embodying love and a servant's heart. Greenleaf (1977) argues, "I believe that the essential quality that sets servant-leadership apart from others is that they live by their conscience-the inward moral sense of what is right and what is wrong" (Kindle location, 94).

Patterson (2015) states, "Servant leadership focuses on your followers." Paterson's description is one of the most salient and powerful disciplines of the servant leader. Focusing on followers is what Jesus did in the upper room. Jesus was physically and spiritually cleansing the disciples and serving their need on a night when he had every right to be served, and have his followers focus on his needs. Northouse (2013) states, "Leaders have an ethical responsibility to attend to the needs and concerns of followers" (Kindle location, 484). What Northouse calls an ethical responsibility, I would call an ecclesial responsibility. Additionally, I would define followers against the backdrop of future followers, or in the church world, future disciples.

On one occasion, Jesus heard the request of the mother of James and John in Matthew 20:20; she requested that each of her sons sit on either side of Jesus when they came into His kingdom. Jesus dismissed the request saying, "Only my Father can give those seats away." When the other ten disciples heard what she asked, there was a staff scuffle. All of the disciples had thought about the position, but none of their mothers had the gall to ask Jesus for this. Now there was a holier-than-thou argument ensuing over this mishandled request. Jesus shut down the argument with the juxtaposition between servant leadership and the positional leadership.

Jesus stated,

> "You know that the rulers of the Gentiles lord it over them, and their high officials exercise authority over them. Not so with you. Instead, whoever wants to become great among you must be your servant, and whoever wants to be first must be your slave— just as the Son of Man did not come to be served, but to serve, and to give his life as a ransom for many (*Matthew 20:25-27, NIV*).

Jesus transitioned the disciple's position-oriented leadership framework to servant leadership framework when He says, "Not so with you." You are not like the world. You are not like positional leaders; rather you are to be a servant leader. You do not become great through position but through submission. You do not become great by where you sit, but rather from where you serve. Leadership is a verb, not a noun; it is active, not passive, and it is follower oriented not leader-centric. Jesus contrasted the hierarchal leadership style and the servant leadership style, highlighting the heart and motive behind servant leadership instead of emphasizing power and position as the end to the means from the hierarchical style.

Patterson's (2003) consideration of the approaches, principles, and behaviors of leaders led her to see seven attributes of the leader-follower servant leadership model: Patterson, list, (a) Agapao love, (b) humility, (c) altruism, (d) vision, (e) trust, (f) empowerment, and (g) service." The level of these attributes that are actively working with the leader to lead transformation in the follower will determine the level of effectiveness in which a servant leader is operating. Love is foundational and formative.

Humility demands the focus be removed from the leader and be turned to the need of the follower. Altruism tests the motives of the individual leading. The great litmus in understanding the level of altruism is asking, am I doing this to get something for my followers from them?

Vision determines where you intend to take the followers. Your direction determines your directives. Trust is like a bank account when you are a little kid. At first, you may start off with some money from your parents to open the account. At some point, you have to begin to make deposits. That is where understanding the dynamics of trust evolves. Position may initially give you some trust. However, the wise servant leader will immediately go to work making deposits in that personal account and investing in people. When you add value to people, and you recognize their value, then you are building trust. Trust is built daily, not in a day. However, trust can be withdrawn in a day if the leader is immoral or emotionally inconsistent.

Empowerment happens when the leader does not care who receives the credit.

Next is empowerment. Empowerment is divesting you of your power, delegating that power to your followers, and systematically building or investing into their lives to help them succeed at the designated task. Empowerment is the selfless leader hogging the blame while being generous with the credit. Empowerment understands Blanchard and Bowels (2001) notion that, "None of us are as smart as all of us." If a leader is empowering, he or she is more concerned with effectiveness than selfishness. This strong attribute is significant to a servant leader.

The final attribute of the servant leader is service. The servant leader should ask his or herself, what am I doing that is a service to my followers? If my followers are servicing my needs, then I am not a servant leader. If, however, I am providing service to my followers that improves their lives and helps them succeed, then I am fulfilling this attribute of being a servant leader.

Serving Your Community

Understanding the origin and the elements of servant leadership, you can now focus on the community in which God has placed you. According to scripture, "Your steps are ordered of the Lord" (*Psalms 37:23*). When growth is not happening, it is easy to begin to question, is God really with me? Am I truly called to this city? These questions lure your emotions into a whirlwind of doubt and despair, just before dropping you down to the ground again.

For God to revitalize your church, you must believe with all of your being that God had placed you there strategically. Jesus stated, "No one lights a lamp and puts it in a place where it will be hidden, or under a bowl. Instead, they put it on its stand, so that those who come in may see the light" (*Luke 11:33, NIV*). God is the one that lit you on fire. He did not place you where you would be ineffectual and feckless; instead, he placed you on your stand. Notice the word "its." "Its" is possessive of the light. Likewise, God has a stand for you. It is right where he placed you, therefore, let your light shine.

As you turn your eyes to your city, start with a prayer and fasting emphasis. During this season of seeking and hearing from God on how to serve your city, ask the Holy Spirit, the ultimate Church growth strategist, how can you contextualize serving your community? The Holy Spirit will place methods and mandates in your heart about how to accomplish His goals. You may study how others serve their city and connect with the heart of the community. Don't just copy and paste someone else's strategy into your setting; take everything you see and ask how we could synthesize and customize their strategy and improve this?

Have you been "VIPped?"

We developed a concept many years ago that was quite effective. It's called VIP. We wanted to let every person with whom we came in contact know they were a very important person to God and a very important person to us.

The acrostic obviously stands for "Very important person." That was the heart of everything that was done out of the VIP emphasis.

We coined the words "VIPped" and "VIPping." The church had these attractive business cards printed; on the front, it said: "You have been VIPped?" On the back it said, "You are a very important person to us, and to God, to find out what it means to be "VIPped" go to this link." The card included a link to a page on our website that explained why they were important to God and us, and we would love to have them as our guest at the next church service.

Next, we encouraged people to VIP people at work, in their neighborhood, and out in the community. Many people would buy someone's coffee in the drive-through line and leave a VIP card. Some would pray that Jesus would lead them to pick up the check for a table in a restaurant and instead of receiving a bill they receive a VIP card. Other's found an elderly person's yard that needed to be raked and "VIPped" them. "VIPping" is any random act of kindness that sends the message you are important to God and us.

"VIPping" is encouraged individually, during a season of emphasis leading up to Easter or just before school starts. Christmas is also a good time; however, people tend to have less discretionary resources around this time. By choosing a time each year to reemphasize this initiative, you can build on memories and momentum especially by telling the stories of people who have been "VIPped" who are now active parts of your church.

One year we even did a mystery campaign wherein we put up billboards that said, "Have you been 'VIPped?'" This campaign engaged our people and drove them to "VIP" even more. It also caused the curious to look into the church much more than just an ordinary billboard.

Not only did we encourage individual "VIPping," but we modeled this style of servant leadership on a larger scale by serving those who serve the community. At key times throughout the year, we would "VIP" different public servant departments. We have held barbecues for the police department, the fire department, the sheriff's office, and other key community service groups. These were phenomenal ways to show appreciation and to get the church into the community doing what she does best, loving people. As a result of these VIP events, we have had entire families come to know Jesus and plug into the life of our church.

Another form of VIP events was our VIP Backyard. We identified people in our church with properties conducive to hosting a larger event. We scheduled these backyard events to happen during the weeks before school starting in August. Our goal was to create a high-end event that would make church members proud to invite their friends.

We had black-tie service teams from the church who served on linen-covered tables outside on the lawn. We had church people prepare hors-d'oeuvres that were brought out in serving rounds, along with a self-serve chocolate bar outside. Additionally, our worship band learned some classic songs and performed live which capped off the experience. The goal was for our people to serve at one party and invite to the next party. By serving at a party and then attending and inviting people to the next, this kept people from getting burned out, and they enjoyed both ends of the experience. The fact is friends of the people in your church will come to a high-end backyard party much quicker than they will a church service. Once these VIP guest arrived, the hope was that they would meet our amazing people, see excellence, build relationships and be ready to respond to an invitation to church. The invitation to church was especially easy after the church people told their friends that the band playing was the Sunday morning worship band.

I became a lead pastor in 2001. Since then, I have led our churches to engage and serve the less fortunate in our cities in a variety of ways. We just opened a non-prophet called City Interactive with the goal of setting up five City Interactives in various parts of under resourced Memphis. Each City Interactive will meet a unique need of the less fortunate in that area. Why are we doing this? It is a divine directive. If the church cannot have a river of empathy flowing from its praxis then she is anemic, and impotent.

Kerr (2016) states "Empathy, is one of the competencies of emotional intelligence, it is defined as the ability to be aware of, to understand and to appreciate the feelings and thoughts of others." Dr. Kerr outlines an intangible attribute that is latent in the life of the emotional intelligence of a servant leader. Leadership is not merely getting people to move from point A to point B; it is transforming those individuals in the process. When your church sets her eyes on Jesus and develops a heart for her community, then she can empathize with the wealthy and the weak alike.

Ackermann and Eden (2004) state, "Strategic management is about people creating outcomes, not just about outcomes" (p.15). The real commitment to the work of the ministry is formed not when people are told how to think, but when they are empowered to think in line with the Christ-centered goals of the church. When people grapple with the solutions, they own the answers. Therefore, cast a strong vision to serve the community, empower people to be the solution, then release them to thrive. Churches must have what Caligiuri (2012) calls, "Cultural agility. Cultural agility is the mega-competencies that enable professionals to perform successfully in cross-cultural situations" (Kindle location, 304).

Gyertson (2006) states, "Ours is a sacred calling not only to inform but also to model the disciplines of the renewed mind, restored heart and competent, compassionate service with our reformed and reforming hands" (p.9). In ecclesiastical environments, the tandem initiatives to develop the "discipled," and to disciple the developed is paramount for the future posturing of the church. It is in the modeling of these disciplines that broad scale life-transformation takes place.

Gyertson (2009) argues, "Leaders must have a head-first calling anchored to the belief that before the heart can be purified and hands equipped for sacrificial service, the mind must be renewed" (p.5). Discipleship without development can lead to passion without focus; development without discipleship may result in focus without faith. However, when servant leaders leverage their heart and gifts for the focus of expanding the Kingdom of God, then the Kingdom is being built. Blanchard and Hodges (2005) state, "For followers of Jesus, servant leadership isn't an option; it's a mandate" (Kindle location, 492).

Conclusion

Servant leadership is the way Jesus loved, led, and lived. Jesus is the embodied example of a servant leader. It is safe to say that the motives espoused by Jesus were not for self-protection or self-promotion but for the sole benefit of helping others succeed. Helping others win does not always mean that you placate to their improper positions or ineffective work ethics. A true servant leader lays down his or her desire to be liked to speak truthfully and meaningfully into their followers' lives.

Christ compels us to this level and layer of leadership both through his teachings and his life. When Jesus blessed the children, he was modeling the way. When Jesus spoke to the woman at the well, he was modeling the way. When Jesus washed the disciples' feet, he was modeling the way. Every aspect and every element of the life of Christ modeled the way for us to rise to the level of servant leadership. Long before Greenleaf's (2013) definition of servant leadership, starting with, "the natural feeling that one wants to serve, to serve first," Jesus modeled the way for servant leadership.

Servant leadership focuses on the followers, and for the church, her followers must include those who are not yet followers. Turning the heart of the church toward the community and serving people across the spectrum of socioeconomics with the goal of finding a need and meeting it, and finding a hurt and healing it will inevitably create a relevance to your church that your community has not previously had.

Ask questions about Patterson's attributes of servant leadership. Are there areas that need to be developed in your church? If so, make it a module of training, and begin to let your light shine in this much-needed area. What you build will determine how you live.

It is vital for you to contextualize these types of ideas for your community and situation, but all of those concepts came from the Holy Spirit, out of a heart to serve the community. The best ideas are inside of you. The greatest outreaching is yet to be started in your church to serve your community. Be willing to take a risk, to do something different. You have heard it said, "To get something you have never had, you have to do things that you have never done." So, take the lid off. Pray. Dream. Dare to move. When you do, you will see God move on your behalf.

Chapter Nine

Strategic Health

One day I was at an annual meeting for ministers in my particular fellowship. These meetings are church services to minister to the ministers, along with conducting the official business. During one session, the minister in charge of the service said, "If you need healing for anything in your body, step into the aisle, and someone will pray for you." Immediately I felt the Holy Spirit say to me, "Step into the aisle." Have you ever argued with the Holy Spirit? Well, I did. Right in the middle of a sweet time in the presence of God, I began to argue with the inner voice that I knew was the Holy Spirit. *Step into the aisle? Why would I step into the aisle?* The voice that I know so well said it more sternly within, "Step into the aisle and let them pray for healing."

So, I stepped into the aisle. My only hope was that the person who prayed for me did not ask for details as to why I needed healing. While I am waiting for someone to pray for me, I remember thinking to myself, *please don't ask, please don't ask.* The kind brother placed his arm on my shoulder and asked, "How can I help you pray?" "I don't know I said; I just felt like I needed to step into the aisle." The brother prayed a general prayer, all the while I am asking the Lord, why do I need healing? Did I mishear the voice of the Holy Spirit or was there a health issue of which I was unaware?

About a week later I was playing golf with a friend. This golf game was my first time playing since I received my new hip. I was starting to get back into some regular activities. I was back on my motorcycle; I took my son snowboarding. I had made a full recovery. However, I had noticed localized pain around my prosthetic hip.

Varying pain is, unfortunately, my new norm. Most of the time, I could tell if the weather is about to get cold or warm up substantially by a particular throbbing emanating from and around the titanium. I thought this new pain might be another anomaly of pain. However, the morning I got up to play golf, I noticed something different, my hip was warm to the touch. I was alarmed by it but not enough to cancel the golf appointment.

At about the fifth hole, and three lost balls later, I brought up my hip pain, and how it felt warm this morning. My friend said to me, "Are you kidding me? You don't need to be on a golf course right now you need to be at the doctor's office." I agreed that I would call my surgeon as soon as I finished the round of golf, or ran out of golf balls, whichever one came first.

The Mayo Clinic in Jacksonville listened to what was going on and worked me in the next day for an emergency review. The surgeon walked into the room and palpated the area. Initially, he said, "Everything looks normal to me." Then he turned his head toward the nurse and said, "Is that Dr. Switzer outside?" "Yes," she replied. "Have him bring in his sonogram just to double-check this." The doctor came inside with his mobile sonogram machine in tow.

As soon as they placed the sonogram wand on my hip, my surgeon said. "We have a big problem." Then using the sonogram, he guided a needle to a spot in the hip area that was suspiciously shaded. They pulled a sample and sent it off to confirm his suspicion. When the lab came back, my doctor said, "Chris, I don't know how to tell you this, but we are going to have to do an emergency surgery first thing in the morning to remove your new prosthetic hip. There is an infection in the hip, contaminating your blood, and it is deadly!" I overheard the surgeon's assistant tell the doctor that there was no operating room available for the morning. At which point the surgeon said with a raised voice, "I don't care if we have to do surgery at 3 AM, this hip is coming out first thing in the morning, find me a room."

I laid on the examination table in shock, the loud crinkling of the sanitary paper beneath my body was the only thing I heard as my mind began to swirl. This medical emergency was the reason the Holy Spirit wanted me to step into the aisle. Counterfactual questions started to shoot back and forth through my mind. I began to think, *what if I had disobeyed? What if I had not gone golfing with my friend that day? What if Mayo had not been able to take my initial visit for six weeks? What if that specific doctor, the only doctor in that group who travels with a sonogram had not been just outside my door?*

The doctor admitted me immediately to the hospital. Mayo moved people around, and I had my surgery scheduled first thing the next morning. The doctor told me before the operation, "I am going to do my best to clean all the infection out. We are going to replace your hip. If this does not get all the infection, then we will need to remove the hip a third time and leave you without a hip in the hospital for six weeks while we treat the infection." By this time the anesthetic was kicking in, and I was beginning to fade. Every time I woke up after the surgery, I was overwhelmed with disbelief that I was going to have to go through all of that again, and if they did not get all the infection, go through it a third time.

After two days in ICU, I had an unnerving visit from a group of doctors. Three infectious disease doctors came in and said they had not been able to identify the type of infection I had. When a team of infectious disease doctors at Mayo doesn't know what is going on or what type of infection it is, that is a whole new level of trouble. They said, "We are still growing the cultures and cross-examining them with the global database, but as of yet, this strand has not been identified which means we don't know exactly how to treat it." That was not what you want to hear from some of the smartest doctors in the world.

A few days later, they did identify the strand of infection and reported to me that I would have to be on antibiotics for the rest of my life. Mayo placed a peripherally inserted central catheter or PICC line in my arm. This is a catheter that goes straight into the heart. Twice a day for the next eight weeks I would have to get powerful customized antibiotics that went straight to my heart.

In addition to the PICC line, I had to go back to full-time rehab in order to be released to go home. One day I woke up in a dark depression. I felt evil at the foot of my bed. It happened on a Sunday, and I was supposed to be preaching the Word of God in three services, but instead, I was laid up in bed, struggling through pain and now depression. The physical therapist rolled me to the therapy room and put me on a machine. I could not stop the tears from flowing. One by one they rolled off my cheeks onto my hospital gown. The therapist said, "Let me just take you back to your room," as if to say, I am not that kind of therapist. I prayed, I worshipped, I watched some encouraging preachers on television, and kept plodding on, but the dark depression lingered like a cloud of dust on a windless day. Finally, the Holy Spirit said to me "Turn on Joel Osteen." So I turned the TV on and sure enough, there was Joel. I have spent a little time with Joel, and he is just as sincere in person as he is on television. But that day as soon as I tuned in Joel looked straight into the camera and said, "This is not how your story ends. This is just a coma in a sentence that God is still writing. God is not through with you; your greatest days of ministry are in front of you. The devil has not won, God has made you more than a conqueror and you are going to conquer this."

Although he was speaking to millions at that moment, he spoke directly into the darkness of my soul, and the depression blew away as I felt the wind of the Spirit settle in that hospital room.

Staph Infection

It turns out the infection was a peculiar type of staph infection from the first surgery. This infection had grown in my body to the point that it would have taken my life very soon, if left untreated. As we discuss strategic health, I wonder if there are any infections in the body of the church that are life-risking or in the case of 4000 churches per year in the United States, taking the life of the church. As I write this book one in five churches are protected to close permanently in the next 18 months.

Infections occur when viruses, bacteria, or other microbes enter your body and begin to multiply. Drexler, (1970) notes, "Microorganisms capable of disease pathogens usually enter our bodies through the mouth, eyes, nose, or urogenital openings, or through wounds or bites that breach the skin barrier." Most microorganisms are targeted for destruction by the immune system. However, some intrusions are so powerful that they override the body's formidable natural means of dealing with intruders.

When cells sent to fight the infection begin to die, their last energy is spent sending messengers to other cells for reinforcement. The dying cells not only send a message of urgency, location of the infection but also send message proteins with samples of the invading forces. Then a Dendritic cell carries the samples to the lymph nodes to create customized solutions aboard what is called Helper-T cells. Once created, these cells travel back to the infection site, and bond to other cells and begin to multiply the customized antibodies to attack the invading forces. If these cells win the fight, some cells convert into memory cells to create an immunity in your body toward that invader (Brodsky, 2017).

The war between the antibodies and the infection is so intense that it produces heat at the site of the infection. (Harding, 2016). In spite of all of this fantastic design by a brilliant Creator, there are some infections that are so powerful and multiply so rapidly; the body cannot keep pace with the destructive force of the infection. As a result, sickness and even death can ensue. This heat is what I felt the morning I played golf.

Staff Infection

The same thing can happen in a church. Like our physical body, the body of the church has powerful immune systems that intuitively fight off foreign bodies that seek to make the body of Christ sick and even cause death. Paul, the Apostle to the Gentiles, writes to the church at Ephesus, "For our struggle is not against flesh and blood, but against the rulers, against the authorities, against the powers of this dark world and against the spiritual forces of evil in the heavenly realms" (*Ephesians 6:12, NIV*). Here, Paul is pulling back the veil of battles within the church.

Often, we associate problems within the church with competing ideologies. One faction believes the church should be all about evangelism the other group believes the church should be all about discipleship. Some argue the church needs to hold on to traditional music, while others believe that the Holy Spirit is incapable of moving through outdated music. Competing ideologies is problematic to the extent that they distract the church from the real enemy. All awhile lines are being drawn, and sides are being taken like an infectious disease, problems are multiplying in the body of Christ, and people are blindly falling into an eternity without Christ.

In the church, common ground is the key antibody that displaces the enemy's tactics. Can the prospective opinions concede that the church's purposes are evangelism, worship, discipleship, fellowship, and ministry? Can the factions agree that we are the light of the world? Can the factions agree that the church has the only antidote for the millions of people in our country and billions around the globe that will perish eternally without the life-giving message of the Gospel?

When your body is sick, it is working overtime to kill the virus or bacteria. So much energy is being excreted under the skin to build immunity against the foreign body. All this spent energy is the reason your body is more tired when you are sick because, under the surface, copious energy is being focused on destroying the thing that is trying to destroy you.

The same is true in the body of Christ. If the enemy can keep warring factions within the church, it will cause so much energy to be spent to fight a differing idea or an alternative opinion that the body will be rendered useless and tired much like your body when you are sick. It is in this chronic spiritual fatigue that the body begins to shut down to stay alive.

When I say staff infection, the notion is not that the decline and plateauing trends in the United States are the faults of the staff. While it is true, some staff members become lazy, entitled, unfocused, and ineffectual, the vast majority of pastors want their ministries to grow. They want their churches to thrive. If you are a staff member of a church and you do not have a sense of urgency about the lost, if you do not have a sense of compassion toward the broken, this is a definite call to repent. You need to fast and seek the face of God. Review Jesus' affirmations and corrections of the churches in the book of Revelation and begin to live your life on mission.

You must, as Jesus said, "Consider how far you have fallen! Repent and do the things you did at first. If you do not repent, I will come to you and remove your lampstand from its place" (*Revelation 2:5, NIV*). The day will come when we will all stand before the Maker of all creation and be forced to give an account of the things done on this earth. Paul declared, "For we must all appear before the judgment seat of Christ, so that each of us may receive what is due us for the things done while in the body, whether good or bad" (*2 Corinthians 5:10*). This Judgment is not the Great White Throne Judgment for unbelievers. This judgment is the Judgment Seat of Christ.

James, the half-brother of Jesus, states, "Dear brothers and sisters, not many of you should become teachers in the church, for we who teach will be judged more strictly" *(James 3:1, NIV)*. There is no doubt that irresponsible church staff will face accountability for laziness, apathy, and misdirection. Most leaders were called to the ministry for altruistic purposes and as a result of the Holy Spirit's drawing. However, even the Apostle Paul states, "It is true that some preach Christ out of envy and rivalry, but others out of goodwill" *(Philippians 1:15, NIV)*.

There is some church staff whose motives are impure and are influenced by worldly desires. However, God knows how to use wrong motives to advance the gospel. Paul writes, "But what does it matter? The important thing is that in every way, whether from false motives or true, Christ is preached. And because of this, I rejoice. Yes, and I will continue to rejoice," *(Philippians 1:18, NIV)*. Paul says because Christ is preached, that he will rejoice, and continue to rejoice. However, the bacteria that creates the most sickness in the church is the distraction. When the church takes her eyes off her mission which is to make Hell smaller, then she begins to waste loads of vital energy on infighting, and factions become more concerned with being right than being effective.

The enemy leverages three deadly distractions toward the body of Christ; sin, an internal focus, and division in a church. Sin can be commission or omission; the sin of commission is doing what you know not to do. The sin of omission is not doing what you know to do. Whether by omission or commission, sin is an infectious disease that threatens the body of Christ. Scripture is clear that it brings death. Omission, on a corporate level in the church, takes place when the missiology does not line up with the methodology.

When a church proclaims to preach the gospel however in the last calendar year there has been little effort or money spent to reach the lost in their community. Omission church-wide takes place when there is contentment as long as the bills are paid, and the pet programs maintained. Omission happens when there is a lack of compassion for the poor and passion for prayer.

Omission occurs when success is defined by a rubric of great comfort rather than the Great Commission.

The second deadly distraction in the body of Christ is an inward focus. An inward focus is natural for sinners, but it should be unnatural as believers. Jesus has called the church not to be natural but to be supernatural. Of the five purposes of the church, discipleship and fellowship are the only inward elements. When the whole focus of the church is turned from the one that is lost to the ninety-nine on the hill (Matthew 19:12, NIV), then the back door and front doors of the ministry are closed. In the human body, this would be the medical equivalent of being sick but not take in any food or vitamins to fight the sickness. In an ironic lie from the enemy the thing that seems like it will cost you more, reaching the lost and pulling back those who have wondered, is the very thing needed to reverse the trend, gain strength and momentum and begin to build again.

Hofstede, Hofstede & Minkov (2010) state, "One of the reasons why many solutions do not work or cannot be implemented is that differences in thinking among the partners have been ignored" (Kindle location, 301). Alignment to create a shared picture of the desired future, and the strategies by which to achieve that future is central to aligning individual values with corporate objectives. Without this alignment, the body is spending all its energy fighting on the inside. Kouzes and Posner (2012) state, "Leadership is not about who you are; it's about what you do" (p. 15). The church is spending so much time fighting who they are; they have failed to focus on what they do.

The third deadly distraction is division. Scripture is replete with warnings against divisiveness. Paul wrote to the Romans, "I appeal to you, brothers, to watch out for those who cause divisions and create obstacles contrary to the doctrine that you have been taught; avoid them. For such persons do not serve our Lord Christ, but their appetites, and by smooth talk and flattery they deceive the hearts of the naive" (*Romans 16:17-18, NIV*).

Additionally, Paul wrote to Titus while establishing ecclesial protocols in the first-century church, "But avoid foolish controversies, genealogies, dissensions, and quarrels about the law, for they are unprofitable and worthless. As for a person who stirs up division among you, after warning him once and then twice, have nothing more to do with him, knowing that such a person is warped and sinful; he is self-condemned" (*Titus 3:9-11*). If you're a parent and ever wondered about the origin of counting to three, it was introduced by the Apostle Paul. He notes that someone who instigates and propagates division should only get two chances before the leadership disassociates with them.

What Paul intuitively knew is that the energy wasted in a division is the energy needed to reach lost people, and it prepares those who are saved to do the work of the ministry. When energy is squandered on division, the body does not have the spiritual energy to fulfill its God-given mission. Never underestimate the power of one seed of division.

For me, it was one microorganism that infected the surgical wound, that tried to kill me. That tiny living organism began to multiply; my body was trying to keep up with the intrusion by going through all its natural processes. However, the fact remains, had the doctors at Mayo not caught it in time, I would likely not be telling you this story, and warning you of the power of foreign actors in the body of Christ.

Churches are dying left and right in the United States. These are not bad churches; they are simply churches that are unhealthy. More than 250,000 people die annually in the United States from sepsis (Hershey and Kahn, 2017). Sepsis, or blood poisoning, is on the top ten lists of mortal diseases in the United States. Just like God in his amazing grace, had me in the right place at the right time. He has you, and your church in the right place at the right time to get the help you need to spoil the plans of the enemy.

How Does Your Church Achieve Strategic Health?

Strategic health is a holistic process wherein all the influencers of the church agree to target deadly distractions.

It is in the common ground that you find the sacred ground.

The church should declare a fast. I mean this literally and meta-phorically. The spiritual and physical benefits of fasting food or certain types of food for a season for the purpose of cleansing your body is widely understood. Physically, in the United States, we are reliant on sugar. Several days without sugar and preservatives cleanses your body and causes a reboot of your metabolic system. Spiritually, a fast is a time to die to yourself and focus on all of your beings on the things of God.

The same is true in the church. For a church that has been infighting and has had deadly distractions and warnings on the inside, it is vital that the members of that body die to their selves so that there will be a renewal of the wineskins within (*Luke 5:36-39*). A period of cleansing from sin and an internal focus and division will reboot the powerful systems of the body of Christ, thus spending the natural energy of the body on elements that are essential for the expansion of the gospel.

Conclusion

A thorough review of the post COVID declining and pla-teauing churches in the United States will reveal a devastating trend that can no longer be ignored. Combine this trend with the spiritual disengagement trends of the emerging generations, and it will be clear that a super trend of church closures is only set to escalate. While there are a lot of great church planting movements working feverishly to offset this reality, the closure rate far exceeds the church planting rate. It is for this reason that *The Post COVID Church* dives right into the middle of that trend and is empowering leaders to leverage their God-given gifts and the acumen of strategic leaders to help churches revitalize.

The journey begins with understanding and admitting that the *church is in fact limping*. This trend of decline is often disregarded because of the emergence of the megachurch. Some will argue, churches are growing. While it is true that many churches are posting growth, more churches than not are in decline or have plateaued. Even the mega churches have struggled to come back after COVID. The pain in the walk of many churches is not mitigated by the pre-COVID numerical growth of a few mega churches. There is a lot that can be learned from mega-churches such as their focus, their commitment to excellence, their desire to reach the lost. However, it is more tempting for church leaders to criticize the growth of a megachurch than to learn from it. As with my journey to health, it started by admitting there was a problem, and not ignoring the pain.

When change is needed, the most important activity is to *review your history*. As you examine the history of a struggling church, you will find a treasure trove of Christ-centered, purpose-fulfilling values that must be reviewed and at times rediscovered. By reminding those who may be resistant to making change of the history of the church and focusing on principles and not preferences those who would have had an entrenched mentality, will emerge with a fresh perspective of the core values that are central to the church's purposes.

Next, the church leadership must take an honest *evaluation* of its current condition. Take the vitals. What are the systems of the church telling you about the health of the church? If the church stays on the current trajectory, how long will it last?

Sobering discussions like these are essential to turning the corner from retreat to revive. Feedback must come from all possible sources during this phase to provide a proper assessment. When the pain of decline begins to change the personality of the church and its relationship to the community, then it is time to change.

The next phase is *formulating a 12-month missional calendar*. Refusing to fall prey to the attractional-only camp or the missional-only camp "Refocus" embraces a healthy hybrid of the two. Part of that hybrid is placing a missional "cast" on the functionality of the church. This process forces growth in the thinking of the church as it relates to being missional. The calendar mandates measurable deliverables about missional elements throughout the year. The missional calendar, combined with a strategic preaching and or teaching calendar will carve out a new way of thinking. Creating small victories in the missional department will deliver momentum, that the church has not had previously. That momentum if directed toward the objectives derived from the values and leveraged by the strategies of the church, will take on a life of its own.

The next phase is to *revisit your church culture objectively.* Culture is king. If you as a church leader do not manage your culture, then your culture will manage you. The most significant strategy in the world will be resorbed by a latent culture. Culture change is not easy, but it is necessary for the church to turn the corner from regression to revitalization. Existing culture drives your behavioral norms. If the outcome is going to change for the church, there must first be changes in the culture of the church.

Incrementalism is the best strategy for lasting culture change.

The next phase is to *create a new look.* Those who have disengaged with the ministry, either on the inside of the church or in the community in which you serve, will have a reason to take a new look at the ministry. Often new looks whether online or onsite can serve as a guidepost to stimulate reengagement and organizational commitment from those within but will also garner attention from new prospects. Find one or two places where your efforts and money can go a long way in the areas that are most appreciated. The return on your investment in the right area will far outweigh the related cost.

Undergoing training is the next phase of the "Refocus" process. There are three legs to the stool of this stage upon which church revitalization sits. Design thinking starts with the values, funnels through the objectives, and reviews the strategies to determine what learning, training, or development needs to be for the stated goals to be met. The next leg is becoming a learning organization. A learning organization begins with humility and the understanding that it has not arrived, and as such it must become hungry for aspects and elements that make other churches successful and explore what works in your unique context. A Learning organization is an entity that views learning as part of its ongoing objectives. This learning causes the church to grow from the inside out. The final leg of the stool is leadership development. Leadership development is the deliberate and ongoing measurable path in which an organization builds its future through growing its leaders. These three legs form a stable substratum for the future internal growth of the church, which will inevitably result in numerical growth.

The final phase is *serving the community*. It is vital for leaders to understand what a servant leader is, and where the model originated. The original servant leader gave His life for the freedom of His followers. It is from this heart for followers that true servanthood arises. After understanding the foundations and attributes of a servant leader, the church needs to approach its community through that lens.

Find a need and meet it, find a hurt and heal it.

This adage should be the driving motto for the posture of the church toward the community. When the church approaches the community through servant leadership, she is mirroring the majesty of the Maker. The most effective reflection the church can have to reach the world, is the image of Jesus Christ.

Strategic health understands the intruders of the enemy, and just how tragic an infection of deadly distractions can be.

Strategic health keeps a constant check on its values or the "why," its objectives, or the "what," and its strategies, or the "how."

A church that has strategic health has defined what progress means and has clear, measurable methods that are continually being improved to meet those objectives. A church that possesses strategical health and performs check-up against the backdrop of biblical success and other measurable parameters will remain strategically healthy.

You may feel you are in an impossible situation to turn your church around. The good news is that He is the God of the impossible. God has called you where you are. He wants your church to be the light that led the lost to life in Christ.

When we dare to pray extraordinary prayers on a regular basis, God will do extraordinary things on a regular basis.

The will of God is clear from Scripture. Peter wrote, "The Lord is not slow in keeping His promise, as some understand slowness. Instead, He is patient with you, not wanting anyone to perish, but everyone to come to repentance *(2 Peter 3:9, NIV)*. God does not want one person to perish. Not one. If you are a parent, imagine if I asked you which of your kids you are willing to live without and be ok. You must decide which child you would no longer see. Impossible, right? That is the way God feels about all His children. He does not want one of them to perish. He has left the church here to do her job. The Church's job is to bring glory to God while bringing people to God's glory. If the church is only doing one of those things, then she is not doing her job.

Let an urgency rise within you. The church is going to have to make some changes, and the church is going to have to change. However, the alternative, death, is not an option. Together we can turn the tide of church decline by becoming a strategically healthy church.

There is a powerful metaphor for the church today found tucked away in 2 Kings. If you have ever had a bad month, these guys could relate. They were weighing their final options because none of them looked good. They said to each other, "If we say, 'We'll go into the city the famine is there, and we will die. And if we stay here, we will die. So, let's go over to the camp of the Arameans and surrender. If they spare us, we live; if they kill us, then we die" *(2 Kings 7:4, NIV)*. What these guys did not know was that God had already conquered the enemy. All they had to do is to go into the enemy's territory, face their fears, and they would receive the bounty of a victor.

The same is true for the church. You may be weighing your options, and none of them sound good. You can lay there and do nothing, and the church will die, or you can get up, and go into the enemy's camp. Go to the places in your city that are in need. Face your fears. Move. Get up. When you do God will match your faith with his faithfulness, then you will receive an unexpected harvest from an inconspicuous place. When your church refocuses on its mission, it has the power to go into the camp where the enemy has been and obtain a plunder of purpose, a plunder of lost souls, and a plunder of blessings.

References

Ackermann, F., & Eden, C. (2011). *Making strategy: Mapping out strategic success.* Los Angeles, CA: SAGE Publishing.

Anderson, L. (1997, January 2). Argyris and Schön's Theory on Congruence and Learning. Retrieved from http://www.aral.com.au/resources/argyris.html

Baldoni, J. (2003). *Great communication secrets of great leaders.* New York, NY: McGraw Hill Professional.

Bekker, C. J. (n.d.). Leading with the head bowed down: Lessons in leadership humility. *Inner Resources for Leaders*, 1-10.

Berkun, S. (2007). *The myths of innovation.* Sebastopol, CA: O'Reilly Media. [Kindle]. Retrieved from Amazon.com.

Bersin, J. (2013, March 20). *How Corporate Learning Drives Competitive Advantage.* Retrieved from https://www.forbes.com/sites/joshbersin/2013/03/20/how-corporate-learning-drives-competitive-advantage/#46526f2617ad.

Blanchard, K., & Bowels, S. (2001). *High five: The magic of working together.* New York, NY: Harper Collins.

Blanchard, K., & Hodges, P. (2005). *Lead like Jesus* (2nd ed.). Nashville, TN: W Publishing Group.

Branson, M. L., & Martinez, J. F. (2011). *Churches, cultures, and leadership: A practical theology of congregations and ethnicities.* [Kindle version]. Downers Grove, IL: IVP Academic.

Brown, T., & Katz, B. (2009). *Change by design: How design thinking transforms organizations and inspires innovation* (1st ed.). New York, NY: Harper Business.

Burke, W. W., & Noumair, D. A. (2015). *Organization development: A process of learning and changing* (3rd ed.). Upper Saddle River, NJ: Person Education.

Burton, R. M., Obel, B., & DeSanctis, G. (2011). *Organizational design: A step-by-step approach* (2nd ed.). New York, NY: Cambridge University Press.

Canton, J. (2015). *Future smart: Managing the game-changing trends that will transform your world* [Amazon Kindle version] Philadelphia, PA: Da Capo Press.

Cameron, K. S., & Quinn, R. E. (2011). Diagnosing and changing organizational culture: Based on the competing values framework. San Francisco, CA: Jossey-Bass.

Catmull, E. (2014). *Creativity: Overcoming the unseen forces that stand in the way of true inspiration.* New York, NY: Random House.

Chanack. (n.d.). Retrieved November 21, 2017, from *http://biblehub.com/hebrew/2596.htm*

Chand, S. R. (2011). *Cracking your church's culture: Seven keys to unleashing vision and inspiration.* San Francisco, CA: Jossey-Bass.

Collins, J., & Porras, J. I. (2002). Built to last: Successful habits of visionary companies. Pymble, Australia: Harper Business.

Collins, J. (2001). *Good to great: Why some companies make the leap... and others don't* (2nd ed.). Pymble, Australia: Harper Business.

Cross, N. (2011). *Design thinking: Understanding how designers think and* work. Oxford, UK and New York, NY.

Davila, T., Epstein, M. J., & Shelton, R. D. (2006). *Making innovation work: How to manage it, measure it, and profit from it.* Upper Saddle River, NJ: Wharton School Pub.

DDT and its derivatives, *Environmental Health Criteria Monograph No. 009,* Geneva: World Health Organization, 1979.

Drexler, M. (1970, January 01). *How Infection Works*. Retrieved November 30, 2017, from https://www.ncbi.nlm.nih.gov/books/NBK209710/.

Ford, L. (1991). *Transforming leadership: Jesus' way of creating vision, shaping values and empowering change*. Downers Grove, IL: InterVarsity Press.

Gabler, N. (2006). *Walt Disney*. New York, NY: Alfred A. Knopf.

Gino, F., & Staats, B. (2015, November 1). *Why Organizations Don't Learn*. Retrieved from https://hbr.org/2015/11/why-organizations-dont-learn.

Greenleaf, R. K. (1977). *Servant leadership: A journey into the nature of legitimate power and greatness*. Yahweh, NJ: Palest Press.

Gyertson, D. J. (2006). *Heads first, hearts fast and hands outstretched: A personal theological journey into whole person discipleship*.

Gyertson, D. J. (2009, December 1). *I believe in the Holy Spirit: one Pilgrim's response to contemporary beliefs about and practices attributed to the work and ministry of the Holy Spirit*. DJGyerton.com.

Hamel, G. (2002). *Leading the revolution: how to thrive in turbulent times by making innovation a way of life*. New York, NY: Plume Book.

Harding, D. M. (2016, December 02). *Wound infection | Health*. Retrieved November 30, 2017, from https://patient.info/health/wound-infection#nav-2.

Heiting, G. (2014, March 08). *Myopia control - A Cure for nearsightedness?* Retrieved from http://www.allaboutvision.com/parents/myopia.htm.

Hershey TB, Kahn JM. *State sepsis mandates a new era for regulation of hospital quality*. N Engl J Med [Internet]. 2017 May 21 [cited 2017 June 15]; 376:2311-2313. Available from: https://www.nejm.org/doi/full/10.1056/NEJMp1611928 doi: 10.1056/NEJMp1611928.

Hughes, R., Beatty, K., Dinwoodie, D. (2014). *Becoming A Strategic Leader: Your Role in Your Organization's Enduring Success.* San Francisco, CA: Jossey-Bass.

Jackman, M., and C. Johnson. *Leadership: A communications perspective.* 6th ed. Long Grove, IL: Waveland Press, Inc., 2013.

Jones, T. H. (2016). *Recalibrate your church: how your church can reach its full kingdom impact.* Renton, WA: Recalibrate Group.

Kerr, B. (2016, August 9). *For leaders: sixteen ways of developing empathy.* Leader Development Institute, 10(5). Retrieved from http://www.leadershipdevelopmentinstitute.net/for-leaders-sixteen-ways-of-developing-empathy/.

Kouzes, J. M., & Posner, B. (2012). *The leadership challenge.* San Francisco, CA: Jossey-Bass.

Kremer, G. R. (1991). *George Washington Carver: In his own words.* Columbia, MO: University of Missouri.

Kumar, V. (2013). *101 Design methods.* Hoboken, NJ: Wiley & Sons.

Liedtke, J. & Ogilvie, T. (2011). *Designing for growth.* New York, NY: Columbia Business School Publishing (978-0-231-15838-1).

Merdrano, C. (2011, September 30). Top 10 Strong Fears. Retrieved from https://listverse.com/2011/09/30/top-10-strong-human-fears/.

Michalko, M. (2001). *Cracking creativity: The secrets of creative genius.* Berkley, CA: Ten Speed Press. (Kindle location, 376).

Michalko, M. (2006). *Thinkertoys: A handbook of creative-thinking techniques* (2nd ed.). Berkeley, CA: Ten Speed Press.

Michelli, J. A. (2007). *The Starbucks experience: Five principles for turning ordinary into extraordinary.* New York, NY: McGraw-Hill.

Myra, H., & Shelley, M. (2005). *The leadership secrets of Billy Graham*. Grand Rapids, MI: Zondervan.

Northouse, P. G. (2013). *Leadership: Theory and practice* (6th ed.). Thousand Oaks, CA: SAGE.

Olson, E. E., & Eoyang, G. H. (2001). Facilitating organization change: Lessons from complexity science. San Francisco, CA: Jossey-Bass.

Orr, James, M.A., D.D. General Editor. "Entry for PARACLETE". "International Standard Bible Encyclopedia". 1915.

Oster, G. (2011). The light prize: Perspectives on Christian innovation. Virginia Beach, VA: Positive Signs Media.

Patterson, K.A. (2003). "Servant leadership: A theoretical model." Unpublished Doctoral Dissertation, Regent University.

Patterson, K. (2015, April 13). Leadership to change the world: Dr. Kathleen Patterson. Retrieved November 28, 2017, from http://www1.cbn.com/video/leadership-to-change-the-world-dr-kathleen-patterson.

Phillips, J. (2012). *Relentless innovation*. New York, NY: McGraw-Hill Professional.

Pink, D. H. (2009). *Drive: The surprising truth about what motivates us* [Amazon Kindle version]. New York, NY: Riverhead Books.

Rainer, T. (2005). *Break out churches*. Grand Rapids, MI: Zondervan.

Rainer, T. (2014). An autopsy of a deceased church. Grand Rapids, MI: Zondervan.

Rima, Samuel D. (2000). Leading from the inside out: The art of self-leadership, 2nd ed. Grand Rapids, MI: Baker Books.

Russell, R. F., & Stone, A. G. (2002). "A review of servant leadership attributes: Developing a practical model." *Leadership & Organization Development Journal,*

Schrage, M. (2000). *Serious Play: How the world's best companies simulate to innovate,* HBP.

Senge, P., Kleiner, A., Roberts, C., Ross, R., & Smith, B. (1994). *The fifth discipline Field Book.* New York: Doubleday.

Schultz, H. (2012, June 5). Starbucks CEO Schultz is All Abuzz. CBS News. ww.cbsnews.com/news/starbucks-ceo-howard-schultz-is-all-abuzz/.

Schultz, H., & Yang, D. (2014). *Pour your heart into it: How Starbucks built a company one cup at a time.* New York, NY: Hachette.

Snyder, N. & Duarte, D. (2008). *Unleashing innovation.* San Francisco: Jossey-Bass.

Stetzer, E., & Dodson, M. (2007). Comeback churches: How 300 churches turned around and yours can too. Nashville, TN: B and H Publishing.

Star, P. (2014, August 15). Education expert: Removing Bible, prayer from public schools has caused decline. Retrieved from https://www.cnsnews.com/news/article/penny-starr/education-expert-removing-bible-prayer-public-schools-has-caused-decline.

Strategy Development. Forbes, 47(6). Retrieved from http://www.forbes.com/sites/lawtonursrey/2014/06/04/14-design-thinking-esque-tips-some-approaches-to-problem-solving-work-better-than-others/#71c4180e7452.

Tennant-Snyder, N., & *Duarte, D. L. (2008).* Unleashing innovation: How whirlpool transformed an industry. San Francisco, CA: Jossey-Bass.

Ursrey, L. (2016, March 12). Why design thinking should be at the core of your business strategy development. Retrieved December 08,

2017, from
https://www.forbes.com/sites/lawtonursrey/2014/06/04
/14-design-thinking-esque-tips-some-approaches-to-
problem-solving-work-better-than-others/.

Vinckeboons, J. & Library of Congress. (1650) *[Map of
California shown as an island]*. [Map] Retrieved from the
Library of Congress,
https://www.loc.gov/item/99443375/.

Williams, R. H. (1999). *Secret formulas of the wizard of ads*. Austin,
TX: Bard Press.

Winston, B. E. (2010, October 10). *The virtue of charity: A
foundation for leadership*. Retrieved November 6, 2016, from
https://regent.blackboard.com/webapps/blackboard/con
tent/listContent.jsp?course_id=_140193_1&content_id=_
5732930_1.

World Health Organization (2005). "Operation Cat Drop"
(PDF). *Quarterly news*. 60: 6. Retrieved, October 4, 2017.

About the Author

Chris, a Texas native, received his undergraduate degree from Southwestern University, his Master's from Southeastern University, and his Doctorate in Strategic Leadership from Regent University, School of Business and Leadership. With over 31 years of ministry experience, Dr. Foster is an engaging communicator of the gospel, with church that has growth by over 400% through the pandemic. Additionally, he serves as a Doctoral Chair and Professor at Southeastern University. He is a father of three, Kash, Cruz, and Eden.

CPSIA information can be obtained
at www.ICGtesting.com
Printed in the USA
LVHW100820271022
731674LV00002B/3/J